THE REALITY OF MANAGEMENT

Other titles available in this series

Available early in 1969

Management Series

THE REALITY OF MANAGEMENT

ROSEMARY STEWART

UNABRIDGED

PAN BOOKS LTD : LONDON
By arrangement with
WILLIAM HEINEMANN LTD
LONDON

First published 1963 by William Heinemann Ltd.
This edition published 1967 by Pan Books Ltd.,
33 Tothill Street, London, S.W.1

330 33151 5
2nd printing 1968

© Rosemary Stewart, 1963

Printed in Great Britain by
Cox & Wyman Ltd, London, Reading and Fakenham

To all the managers whose kind cooperation
in research has made this book possible

Contents

PART TWO   THE JOB

Introduction

THIS BOOK IS addressed to all managers who wish to learn more about their jobs for the practical reason of becoming better managers, and to all students who seek to learn something of the realities of management. It also includes references, and a bibliography that should be useful to the management training officer.

The idea for this book developed during many discussions that followed my visits, as a guest lecturer, to management courses and conferences. These discussions took place with managers at all levels and from many different types of company. They showed two things: first, that there are remarkably few books on management, apart from the purely anecdotal, that most managers do not find either too ponderous, or too theoretical, to be readable; secondly, that managers are interested in descriptions of social research into management practice and problems. (Social research is the study of people, both as individuals and in groups.) Therefore, I decided to try to write a book that I hoped managers would find both readable and useful. The material for it comes from two sources: from the research I have done during the last twelve years, during which time I interviewed over 1,500 managers about their work and problems; and from the works of other students of management.

The aim of *The Reality of Management* is to review what has been written about management in theory against what has been learnt about management in practice; to describe some of the results of social research in management which may be of value to the practising manager; and to do so, briefly, clearly and with a minimum use of jargon. Throughout I shall try to show the differences as well as the similarities of managers' jobs. I shall discuss the manager in his setting – which I shall call situation – working in a particular organization with its own distinctive character and problems; in an industry which differs in some ways from others; and in a particular locality and country where the way in which one manages is influenced by local and national traditions.

I should like to express my thanks to the Department of Economics, Massachusetts Institute of Technology which, by kindly making me a guest from September 1961 to January 1962, gave me the time and the facilities to finish this book. I should also like to thank John H. Smith, lecturer in social science at the London School of Economics and Political Science, for his editorial help.

R.S.

PART ONE

The Organization

The first two chapters describe the organizations within which the manager will have to work. The third looks at the relationship between the organization and the people who make it work: how they modify the formal organization as well as how the organization affects the ways in which they think and act. For those who are uninterested in problems of organization, the first two chapters may be heavy going. They are advised to read the rest of the book first.

1

The Setting for Modern Management

BEFORE THE WAR management was an easier, more intuitive job than it is today. The vast majority of firms had simple organization with few managers. Of course, there was specialization but the division between jobs was often fluid, and the jobs were tailor-made to the individuals available. The sales manager might advise on office management and the works manager might help with the accounts. Relations within management were often informal so that the foreman could go direct to the managing director with a problem. Rules were few. Decisions were made by hunch based on experience.

Today, the same firm, if it has done even moderately well, will be larger and its organization more complex. The number of managers and specialists will have increased at a faster rate than the number of employees, thus contributing to the growth in administrative overheads. The management levels will be more numerous and more clearly defined. Specialization of jobs will have increased; the duties of the job may be described in detail together with the qualifications of the person who would be suitable to fill it. Individuals will be fitted to jobs rather than vice versa. Rules will have developed to cover many aspects of the business, such as who is authorized to spend money, how much and on what, or what provision is made when an employee is sick. These rules will apply to categories of people such as factory managers or manual workers; their application to individuals will depend upon which category they are in.

This brief account of a fair-sized company today could also be used to describe the organization of a hospital, the army or the Civil Service. It is the description of a bureaucracy. This word is not used disparagingly but with the technical meaning given to it by sociologists for a method of organization that has certain characteristics. These are not only widespread today but also appeared in some earlier civilizations, for instance, in the civil service of ancient China.

Bureaucracy makes possible a rational approach to administration. Hence it develops in any large organization that aims at efficiency and continuity. It may seem strange to say that the reason for the development of bureaucracy is its efficiency, when the word 'bureaucratic' is often used as a synonym for inefficiency; but this refers to possible developments within a bureaucracy and not to its basic characteristics. To these we shall now turn because they can help us to understand the setting within which business works today. First we shall give a brief, and rather theoretical, description of these characteristics. Then we shall look at their practical implications for management.

CHARACTERISTICS OF BUREAUCRACY

There are four main ones. The first is *specialization*. This exists among any group of people working together, but it is highly developed in a bureaucracy. The distinctive feature of specialization in a bureaucracy is that it applies to the job rather than the individual, so that the job usually continues in existence when the present holder leaves. This makes for continuity. The functions of the job are defined; therefore, the qualifications of the individual who could fill it are, to some extent, specified. He must have the experience and education required for that post.

The second common feature of all bureaucracies is the *hierarchy of authority* which makes a sharp distinction between the administrators and the administered. In industry it is between management and workers, in the armed services between the officers and the rank and file. Within the ranks of the administrators there are also clearly defined levels of authority. This detailed and precise stratification is very marked in the armed forces and the Civil Service. It is developing in many large companies where both the levels of authority and the rewards at each level are now often codified.

The third characteristic of bureaucracy, the *system of rules*, is closely related to the fourth, *impersonality*, since the aim of the rules is an efficient, and impersonal operation. The rules are more or less stable although, of course, some of them will be changed or modified with time. They can be learned; and knowledge of them is one of the requisites of holding a job in a bureaucracy. The existence of these rules is in marked contrast to organizations which regulate their relationships by individual privilege – which is the sociologist's way of saying they are run on the basis of nepotism and blue-eyed boys.

Impersonality is the characteristic which distinguishes bureaucracy most clearly from other types of organization; such as that based on kinship which is found in primitive societies and, to a lesser extent, in civilized societies, for instance, in some family firms. The allocation of privileges is impersonal in a bureaucracy, so is the exercise of authority which should be in accordance with the rules laid down and not arbitrary. Hence in the more highly developed bureaucracies there tends to be carefully defined procedures for appealing against certain types of decisions – the bureaucracy must not only be impersonal, but must be seen to be impersonal.

It is the demand for impersonality, the operation of the rules without ill-will and without favour, which makes the acceptance of bribes a cardinal sin for the bureaucrat. It is also the reason why unscheduled privilege is viewed with such disfavour and why rules to try to prevent privilege based on favouritism are so carefully developed. This does not of course mean that there are no privileges for officials in a bureaucracy, but what there are must be allocated according to definite rules based on rank or seniority. The transition, from the personal bestowal of privileges at the discretion of senior managers to their allocation according to rule, can be seen in many businesses. Nor is it often an easy one. The exact definition of the levels entitled to certain privileges, such as the use of the executive dining-room, can cause many heartaches among those seeking for the privilege, and headaches among the personnel officers trying to define unquestionable rules for its allocation.

These four characteristics of a bureaucracy, *specialization, a hierarchy of authority, a system of rules* and *impersonality*, have developed, as suggested earlier, because they are the most efficient method yet discovered of running a large and continuing organization. They make for efficiency partly because they ensure the continuity that is essential for any organization that is to last longer than the life of its founder; and partly because they provide, as far as possible, for administration to be carried out on a rational basis by the development of a logical system of rules, of division of work, of qualifications for office, and of defined levels of authority. The scope for human whims is reduced to a minimum.

REASONS FOR THE GROWTH OF BUREAUCRACY

Increasing Size

This is the most important reason. We saw at the start of this chapter that as a firm grows specialization increases, there are more levels of authority, and the need for rules to ensure consistency becomes greater. Size also makes orderly administration essential. Smaller companies may still be run successfully on intuition and drive; in a large company the resulting chaos will be too inefficient.

We tend to underrate the increase in big organizations that has taken place in Britain since the war. (Although we are more conscious of the increase in the number of managers working within a bureaucratic framework.) People often refer to the great predominance of small firms in the British economy; although this is true of their proportion of total firms, the statement is misleading if one is thinking of profits or numbers employed. Relatively speaking, there are very few large companies but they form an important and growing part of the British economy.

Size can be measured in several ways: the number of people employed or the amount of capital invested are the most usual. These measures are often similar, except in companies which need a great deal of capital but few employees, such as in oil refining or cement manufacture. In 1949, it was estimated that the 100 largest British companies earned, in terms of net assets, 25 per cent of the national gross trading profits in manufacturing, building, and distribution. By 1955 their share of total profits had increased to 32 per cent.[1] There are no published figures for the 100 largest companies in terms of employment nor, therefore, for their total number of employees. Some idea of size, in terms of number of employees, is given in a study of the Acton Society, which estimated that in 1956 there were at least 65 companies in manufacturing industry that employed more than 10,000 in the UK; some of these companies also have substantial numbers of employees overseas.[2] Subsequent research showed that by 1960 at least another 10 companies were employing over 10,000. Such was the rate of expansion by growth and mergers in those few years. Between them these 75-odd companies would employ about two million in the UK alone.

Manufacturing companies are only one form of large-scale organization; there is also commerce, the nationalized industries, the Civil Service, the National Health Service, the armed services, and much of local government. Between them these employ about eight million, which means that roughly one-third of the working population is in large-scale organizations. All of which are more or less bureaucratic.

Greater Complexity
This is partly a by-product, and partly a cause of increasing size. It makes a rational, highly specialized organization imperative. Two important contributors to greater

1. Prais, S. J., 'The Financial Experience of Giant Companies', *Economic Journal*, pp. 249–64, Macmillan, London, June 1957.
2. *Management Succession*, p. 3, The Trust, London, 1956.

complexity are: the growth of government regulations and increasing mechanization. The latter also makes for stricter discipline. What has to be done is laid down rather than left to a craftsman's judgement.

Scientific Management Movement

The advocates of scientific management stress rational, prescribed procedures. Hence most of the management consultants are trying to promote bureaucracy – although, if they only thought of the word in its popular sense, they would be horrified to be told so! They advise a carefully planned organization with clearly defined levels of authority; specialized jobs which are limited to one function and which are described in detail. They may go so far in their attempts to prevent any ambiguity, as to advise such detailed job-descriptions that the thirty-sixth responsibility of the production control-manager in a list of fifty-five, is 'Advising and assisting Factory Managers as requested in regard to improvements in the layout of Departments, handling of materials, inter-process storing, etc.'[3]

Demands for Equality of Treatment

This is a different type of reason for the growth of bureaucracy. One which is influenced by the ideology prevailing at that time and place. It can be, and in Britain is, an important factor in increasing bureaucracy. The citizen wants equality of treatment from the Civil Service. Questions in the House try to ensure that he gets it, thereby putting pressure on the Civil Servants to administer strictly in accordance with the rules, so that no questions will be asked. The employee, through his union, strives for the acceptance of rules to ensure that management cannot discriminate. An example is the demand for promotion by seniority, since seniority is easily defined[4] and merit is debatable.

3. Brech, E. F. L., *Organization: The Framework of Management*, p. 167, Longmans, Green, London, (New York) 1957.

4. Although those who have to administer the rules governing promotion by seniority on the railways may laugh at the idea that it is easily defined.

One of the trade unions' reasons for favouring nationalization was that it would give them greater power to enforce their demands for fairness. The history of the nationalized industries shows the way in which such demands can lead to increasing bureaucracy. Fairness is usually identified with equalities of treatment. Hence any variation in the conditions of work in one area of a nationalized industry from the others is likely to be challenged as unfair. If rules and procedures are to be devised which are demonstrably fair by this standard, little or no allowance can be made for local difficulties and preferences.

The power of those who complain of inequality of treatment to bring pressure upon senior officials is important in determining the extent to which rules are made to ensure impersonal treatment. Civil Service rules are the most carefully devised. The nationalized industries, which legally have to consult with their employees on matters directly affecting them, are committed to developing a more carefully defined personnel policy than does private industry. The client and the employee, when they are organized to demand equality of treatment, both exert pressure towards greater bureaucracy. Yet, being human and therefore paradoxical, when these rules are applied to themselves they may complain of bureaucracy, of an unfeeling machine which takes no account of individuals.

LIMITATIONS ON THE GROWTH OF BUREAUCRACY

Why with such powerful forces pressing towards greater bureaucracy is there not even more of it in business today? We know that there are variations in the extent of bureaucracy even though we may claim that 'business is getting more like the Civil Service every day'. Within industry itself there are also great differences in the extent to which bureaucracy has developed; not merely between the large firm and the medium-sized one but between firms of the same size. What are the reasons for these variations and what factors make for more or less bureaucracy? But first what is a more developed bureaucracy? It is popularly equated with the amount of red-tape, yet this, although it may be a by-product, is not a criterion by which one can judge the amount of bureaucracy; one may merely be judging the efficiency of the O and M department! Rather the criterion is the extent to which the four characteristics of bureaucracy have developed.

There are three main limitations on growth of bureaucracy: one, managers' reactions; two, changes in management philosophy, and three, the pressure of rapid change.

Management Reactions

We have seen powerful reasons why managers of large companies should make them more bureaucratic. The extent to which they do so will depend partly on their attitude to management and the kind of people they are and partly on the situation of their companies. Some managers' personalities, the philosophies of management, are opposed to the orderly administration which is characteristic of a bureaucracy. They may find it irksome – even unbearably so – to be bound by rules. They may attach a great value to intuition and initiative. They may prefer to reward where they think fit, paying the salary which they think the man is worth – or which is necessary to attract him, or hold him – and giving him the privileges which they think he deserves with little regard to the post he occupies. They may trust their own judgement in selection and expect the man to mould the job to suit himself, rather than choose a man who fits a job specification. In sum, they may believe that initiative is only fostered in a free-wheeling company, where people have as big jobs as they can make and earn as much as they prove themselves to be worth.

The attitudes and personality of top management will, therefore, influence the amount of bureaucracy in the company. But even if they are opposed to bureaucracy there are, as we have seen, powerful pressures towards it, which makes it difficult for a large company to prosper without a bureaucratic framework. Gradually the managers who are opposed to bureaucracy are replaced by those who are temperamentally in favour of it or who, at least, can adapt themselves to it. Instead of the entrepreneur, there is a career manager who may look to a hierarchy of authority and a system of rules to establish and protect his status.

Changes in Management Philosophy

In the previous section we were concerned with differences in the attitudes and temperaments of individual managers. These are important, but the prevailing management philosophy will also influence management action. In the last few years there has been a partial move away from the mechanistic approach to organization,[5] which prevailed in the inter-war period. Then the emphasis was on the technical advantages to be derived from size and from making use of the most qualified expert. Now there is a greater concern for human reactions, therefore, an awareness of the limitations of a purely rational organization.

Pressure of Change

A company in a rapidly changing situation cannot, if it is to be successful, be very bureaucratic; as jobs change authority relationships become more flexible and many of the rules cease to be appropriate. Therefore, the situation in which the company operates will influence the amount of bureaucracy that is possible. So important is the situation of the company that we shall devote the whole of Part Three to examining its effects.

MANAGERS IN A BUREAUCRACY

We have talked about the reactions of top management to bureaucracy. What about the other managers? What are the implications for the junior and middle manager of working

5. This means treating an organization as if it is a mechanical structure which can be designed, and will operate on purely rational lines, and which can, therefore, be prescribed in advance.

in a bureaucracy; that is, of working in the typical framework of a large company today? It will have both advantages and disadvantages for him; fewer advantages for the manager who is not an 'organization man'. He will be appointed for his qualifications rather than for his connections. The greater the belief in the need for qualifications the smaller becomes the personal element in appointment. This will suit the young manager who is looking for a post and is short of connections. He may be less enthusiastic when he wants to appoint new staff and finds that his freedom is restricted by the appointments procedure.

The manager in a bureaucracy is expected to be loyal to the organization rather than to a person. In return the organization looks after him as long as he fulfils his duties. What is meant by 'fulfilling one's duties' varies considerably, but in some British businesses security of tenure for managers is nearly as great as for the established Civil Servant. Other companies, including some large ones, are not at all bureaucratic in their dismissal of staff. They may even go so far as to dismiss a manager on the spot because he has been judged inefficient. By contrast the senior managers of some other companies may agonize for years before deciding to give a man a handsome, golden handshake.

A bureaucracy also offers its officials an established pattern of career expectations. The continued absence in most businesses of such a career pattern is one of the ways in which business has, so far, remained less bureaucratic than the Civil Service and the armed forces. But there is pressure from the young men, especially the graduates now coming into industry, for more information about their job and salary expectations. So far this pressure has been largely unsuccessful; the young men are still told 'it is up to you'. However, in 1960, Unilever in its advertisements went a little of the way to meet the demand for information about future salaries when it promised newly engaged trainees that they would get £1,100 in three years' time.

One of the great advantages for the manager of working in a bureaucracy is that he is free from much former arbitrariness. He will know much better where he stands in the organization. His responsibilities and authority will be laid down. Good work will be more likely to be rewarded by promotion since bureaucracies try to make an impersonal assessment of merit. Privileges and, to some extent, his pay will be determined by the post he occupies rather than by his standing with the boss. However, the wide flexibility and secrecy of salaries which exists in many companies is another of the ways in which some companies are still un-bureaucratic.

In a bureaucracy greater emphasis is placed on the value of professional skill, on a rational matter-of-factness. This means that the manager must be able to convince others of the correctness of his judgement; being human, their willingness to be convinced will depend partly on whether he gets on well with them. So many leading companies are now looking for men who are intelligent, well-balanced, and acceptable as well as educated. With these characteristics the men should make ideal managers within the bureaucratic framework.

One of the disadvantages for the manager of working in a bureaucracy is that his freedom of action will be curtailed. He will be restricted by the definition of his job's responsibilities and authority. We saw that he benefited from knowing where he stood; but he may suffer from not being able to move from that spot. He is the occupant of a continuing post which has certain duties and privileges attached to it. He must manage within the rules of the organization and accept the limitations on his authority, including his authority over his staff. Some managers will consider these disadvantages a small price to pay for their own security and steady advancement by merit; others may reluctantly adjust to a changed pattern of management. Yet others will choose to work in a less bureaucratic, more free-wheeling company, where their chances of rapid promotion may be greater.

THE PROBLEMS OF BUREAUCRACY

The problems of bureaucracy are the problems of balance. The characteristics, specialization, a hierarchy of authority, a system of rules and impersonality, help to make for efficient and continuing organizations but only if they are not developed to excess. There are two main dangers in bureaucracy: one, that what should only be means become ends in themselves; two, that insufficient allowance is made for different or for changing conditions.

The classic danger in a bureaucracy is of course an over-emphasis on rules; hence the stereotype of a bureaucrat as a man who punctiliously keeps to formal procedures however inappropriate – the man who hoists the flag while the building is burning. The existence of rules inevitably limits flexibility. One reason why 'bureaucratic' is often a slur word is because a bureaucracy is necessarily impersonal in the administration of its rules; it is often accused of inhumanity. Hence one of the problems of a bureaucracy is how to combine the development of impersonal rules which prevent favouritism with sufficient flexibility to deal with the hard case which does not fit the rules. The impersonality of a bureaucracy can be modified by the way in which the rules are devised, so that some latitude is left to the individual bureaucrat in interpreting them to meet a hard case, as well as by the attitude of the administrator himself. Bureaucracies must be impersonal, but the individuals in them can strive to be humane in their interpretation of the rules.

Another obvious danger of bureaucracy is rigidity: hence an inability to adapt fast enough to changing conditions. This is most likely in a company where the managers are used to stable conditions and now find, either because conditions have changed or because they have entered a new and different kind of market, that their old methods are unsuitable. This point will be discussed more fully in the last chapter 'The Manager and Change,' and readers who are interested in a discussion on the 'pathologies of bureaucracy', particularly red-tape and empire-building, are referred to Marshall E. Dimock's *Administrative Vitality*[6] or *Parkinson's Law*.[7]

Yet another potential weakness of bureaucracy is the development of the organization man. Any organization must try to ensure that its members further its objectives and will seek to do so by the use of discipline, incentives, and by encouraging a sense of loyalty to the organization and a devotion to duty. The problem, especially in industry where innovation is often essential, is to do this without developing an organization type to which all newcomers are expected to conform. The dangers of conformity, emphasized in William H. Whyte's widely acclaimed book, *The Organization Man*,[8] are disturbing the Americans, who are busily sponsoring research into 'creativity' in the hope of finding out how to combat them. Again it is a problem of balance, since there will always be a clash between the need for managers to be reliable and the dangers of over-conformity. The top management in each company must assess whether it has the balance right between the advantages of reliability and the limitations of conformity. In weighing the scales it should allow for the fact that judgement is likely to be weighted against the individualist.

The conclusions we may draw from our discussion of bureaucracy are that it is bound to develop in an established and continuing organization which seeks to be efficient. Some degree of bureaucracy is essential for efficient management, the problem is how much? Before management makes its company more bureaucratic, in accordance with the advice of the supporters of scientific management, it should examine the problems of its business now, and in the near future, to see whether doing so is likely to help or hinder efficient

6. *Administrative Vitality: The Conflict with Bureaucracy*, Harper Bros, New York, 1959. (Routledge & Kegan Paul, London, 1960.)

7. Parkinson, C. Northcote, *Parkinson's Law or The Pursuit of Progress*, John Murray, London, 1958. *Parkinson's Law and other studies in administration*, Houghton Mifflin, Boston, 1957.

8. Simon & Schuster, New York, 1956. (Jonathan Cape, London, 1957.)

management. The findings of its examination will depend upon the particular circumstances of the company. What these are, and how they do, and should, influence the organization and behaviour of management will be a recurring subject throughout this book.

SUMMARY

Bureaucracy provides a common setting – and one which we often take for granted – for organizations with different purposes. (We used 'bureaucracy' with its sociological meaning of a particular form of organization, not in its pejorative sense.) The characteristics of a bureaucracy, which these organizations have in common, are: one, *specialization* of jobs which become continuing posts, for which suitably qualified individuals are recruited; two, a *hierarchy of authority* composed of clearly defined levels, with a sharp distinction between the administrators and the administered; three, a *system of rules*; and four, *impersonality*, which is seen both in the administration of the rules and in selection and promotion.

Bureaucracy has developed because it is more efficient than other forms of organization. It makes for rational and continuing administration. The increasing size and complexity of companies encourages the growth of bureaucracy. So does the demand for equality of treatment. Bureaucracy also gains strength from the arguments of the advocates of scientific management who urge the value of a carefully defined, orderly organization. Yet there are limitations on the growth of bureaucracy in business of which the most important are management reactions – top management, in a particular company, may be temperamentally opposed to bureaucracy or believe it to be undesirable; a change in management philosophy towards one which emphasizes the organic, rather than the mechanistic approach to organization; and the effects of rapid change which requires a flexible organization.

For the manager, working in a bureaucracy, there will be advantages and disadvantages. It will suit some temperaments better than others. On the one hand, the manager is freed from much former arbitrariness. He will be appointed for his qualifications and, as far as possible, promoted on merit. He will have an established status with appropriate salary and privileges. He can look forward to a known pattern of career expectations and he will be free from the fear of arbitrary dismissal. His loyalty should be to the organization rather than to individuals. On the other hand, the manager will lose some of his freedom of action. He will be the occupant of a continuing position with prescribed duties and limitations within which he must work. If he is good his speed of advancement may be less than in a more free-wheeling company.

The problems of bureaucracy are the problems of balance: how to have rules which are impersonal but not inhuman, which are fair yet take the individual into account; how to have a structure that is not too rigid to adjust to change; how to have loyal managers who further the organization's objectives without developing into organization men. These problems are inescapable, but they can be ameliorated.

2

What Kind of Structure?

WE SAW IN THE last chapter that the characteristics
of a bureaucracy exist today, to a greater or lesser
extent, in all large companies and in most medium-sized
ones too. Yet they only provide the setting within which the
organization will be designed. An hierarchy of authority
and specialization of jobs are but the beginning. They do
not provide the answer to two of the main problems of organization: how the work is to be divided – both between
posts at the same levels and between different levels;
and how it is to be co-ordinated. Once work is divided there
has to be co-ordination. As Urwick has said: 'The purpose of
organization is to secure that this division works smoothly,
that there is unity of effort or, in other words, coordination.'[1]

The manager will want to know what are the problems in
designing, or changing, an organization and, whether there
is one set of principles which he can use to guide him, in the
same way as an engineer uses the principles of thermo-
dynamics in designing a boiler. If he turns to the writers on
organization for guidance, he will find that they are of two
kinds: the *theorists*, who seek to establish universal principles of how an organization *ought* to work, and the *investigators*, who try to find out how organizations work in
practice, and then see whether this knowledge may lead to
generalizations about the nature of organization. The former have a longer history than the latter. They consist
mainly of managers and consultants. They have developed
the principles of organization which are taught to students

1. Urwick, L., *The Elements of Administration*, p. 44 (first published
1943). Pitman, London (second edition) 1958.

for the Diploma of Management Studies. The latter group is of recent origin. It is research-centred and most of its writers are social scientists. We shall examine the contributions of both groups to see what use they can be to the manager.

This chapter will try to do three things:

To describe the main problems of organization and the kinds of decisions that have to be made in planning the structure.
To give a brief description of the theoretical writing on the subject and its search for principles.
To discuss what has been learnt from the study of how organizations work, and what relevance this may have to the orthodox principles of organization.

Let us now turn to the specific decisions which have to be made in designing an organization, taking first, for ease of illustration, the problems of setting up a new company.

PLANNING THE STRUCTURE

Division of Work

Specialization can be taken for granted, but this does not tell us how the work is to be divided up. In any company there will be some obvious divisions. In a manufacturing company these will be production, sales and finance; but there are other functions which are essential in some industries and for some companies, yet not for others, for instance, research or advertising. Then there is the general question of what tasks the company should do for itself and for what ones it would be more economical to employ outside specialists. Market research or public relations are examples of services which may be wholly or partly farmed out.

In deciding what departments are essential management must consider what are the main objectives of the business: what it is setting up this company to do and what forms of competition will it be meeting? A research department will be vital to a company which is entering a new, expanding and highly technical industry, such as electronics; whereas in many consumer industries, such as cosmetics, detergents or breakfast foods, the sales organization and advertising will be the most important side of the business. The type of customer catered for is also important, for instance, in the consumer trades and services it will determine whether a delivery service and charge-account facilities should be provided. In some industries and companies the main departments may be of about equal importance; in others, the success of the company will be heavily dependent on one department, although, of course, the others must make their contribution too.

To decide that a particular function is necessary is only the first step. Next is the question of how it should be organized. This will be affected by the system of production and the type of market. Hence, two of the most usual methods of division are by product and by area. If a number of different products are to be made, these may be organized as separate production divisions which may operate inside one factory, or each product may be made in a separate factory. Division by area is common on the sales side, especially where the sales force has to deal with a large number of retail outlets scattered over the country. But a company which is selling to a few major customers, whether they are other manufacturers or large chain stores, will have no need of an area sales organization. A company producing a bulky consumer product, such as soft drinks, where transportation costs can be an important factor in selling price, may find it desirable to set up small production units in different parts of the country.

Line and Staff
The work of a company after being divided into the main functions, such as production and sales, is further subdivided into, what are usually called, line or operational and staff or specialist jobs. In designing the structure for a new company, management has to decide which will be line and which staff functions. Line functions are those which have direct responsibility for achieving the objectives of the com-

pany. Staff activities are those which primarily exist to provide advice and service. Whether a function is line or staff should depend on the company's objectives. Research, for instance, is sometimes line when new products and processes are vital for the success of the company, more usually staff when its role is less important. As the company grows larger, management finds it must hive off some of its activities. Then more and more staff jobs are likely to be created, such as market research, personnel and materials handling.

How to establish satisfactory relations between line and staff personnel is one of the most difficult problems of organization. It is difficult because of the possibilities of frustration and conflict which are always present in the relationship. The line manager may feel that his customary and well-tried ways of doing things are being threatened by new-fangled specialists, whose advice he may yet be afraid to ignore. He may become so unsure of his authority that he goes to the staff man on even the smallest matter for a statement of 'Company Policy'. This is a particular danger in industrial relations. Alternatively, the line manager may pay no attention to the staff man who may then feel frustrated by his lack of responsibility and frequent inability to get his ideas put into effect. The relationship is often made more difficult by the specialist's jargon.

Satisfactory relations between line and staff can only be achieved with time, which allows for the growth of mutual confidence. Hence, when management is planning a new organization it cannot provide an answer to the problems of the relations between the two. It can, however, minimize the likelihood of trouble. It should make all vital activities line functions, otherwise staff men in that function will either try to exercise authority or will be unusually frustrated. An example is the research department, which should be line, in a company where research is crucial for success. The organization planners should also keep the specialists as near as possible to the line manager whom they will be serving, so that mutual confidence can have the best chance of developing. Physical proximity is desirable, but, where that is not convenient, good communications are essential.

Levels of Authority

The most important decision to be made now is how many levels of authority there should be. The number of tiers in the management hierarchy vary in practice from two in a small company – the boss and his supervisory staff reporting directly to him – to well over a dozen in some large companies. Size, obviously, makes a difference, but management still has considerable choice as to how many levels to establish. It may opt for as few tiers as possible, on the grounds that this makes for better communication and more responsible jobs. This would require a wide span of control or a group type of company which is divided into a number of smaller, semi-autonomous units. If management is an adherent of the principle of span of control[2] the number of tiers will depend upon the number and type of employees, and upon whether these are divided among subsidiary companies. A company with a large number of manual workers will have fewer tiers than one of the same size with a larger proportion of white-collar workers, because the supervisory ratio is greater on the shop floor (that is, the number of people reporting to the supervisor).

Posts will have to be assigned to the different levels. In planning a new company this may be done by deciding which functions must report to the managing director, and then what activities should report to the senior managers, and so on. In an established company there can be difficulties. If the place of individual managers in the hierarchy has always been hazy, an attempt to state it clearly may upset many people who believed their position to be higher. This problem most often arises when an organization chart is published. It is one reason why some top managers are opposed to organization charts, although they may have

2. The principle of 'span of control', which is discussed later in this chapter, says that a manager should not have more than five or six subordinates, whose work interlocks, reporting to him.

a hand-made copy locked in their desk, as a guide to how they would like the organization to be.

Organization Charts

At this stage in planning, management should decide whether it wants an organization chart and, if so, what kind. It might consider some of the attempts that have been made to draw charts that are more informative than the traditional ones.[3] If its planning has been as methodical as our description, it will probably have roughed out a chart as it went along. The chart helps to show what has been decided. It will also be useful for showing to newly appointed managers and inquiring visitors. But organization charts have their dangers. Their usefulness is often exaggerated and they can rapidly get out of date. All too few organization charts have notes to explain them; without them the reader may make different assumptions about their meaning. He may also be in danger of thinking the reality is as tidy as the chart (in the next chapter we shall see how far the two may be divorced). But the greatest danger is, that unless they are frequently revised, they may so soon give a false picture of even the formal organization. An organization chart can be a useful tool, and an aid to explanations about the organization, but it is often misused. Its very clarity of statement can be misleading.

At this stage in planning an organization the framework is complete, but the task is not finished. If, for instance, top management interviews a potential sales manager and shows him the chart, he might – and should – ask: 'How much responsibility shall I have?' This question would show up two areas which have yet to be tackled. One, what type of decisions should be taken at each level of management – that is, how much decentralization there should be? Two, what should be the responsibilities of each job?

Decentralization

One of the most difficult decisions to be made in planning an

3. cf. Brech, op. cit., pp. 331–41, describes a number of these experiments.

organization is how much decentralization there should be. No business of any size is completely centralized as, if it is to function at all, some decisions must be taken on the spot rather than at the centre. It is not a choice between centralization and decentralization, but of how much decentralization there should be. The answer is likely to vary, from one department to another, according to which decisions top management consider of vital importance to the business. In one company, for instance, all appointments above the £2,000 level may be made by top management. In another, all proposed price changes might have to be referred to top management.

Top management cannot say that it leans towards centralization or decentralization, for so much will depend upon the particular circumstances at the time. What is the best balance between centralization and decentralization may well vary at different periods in a firm's history. In a new company, or in an amalgamation of two or more companies, greater centralization will be necessary in the early stages so as to establish common policies, where these are desired. A common management tradition will make greater decentralization possible because managers will tend to think and act in the same way. The amount of decentralization which may be desirable will also be influenced by the calibre of junior and middle management – hence the freedom of decision that can safely be allowed them; the type of decisions that have to be taken; and the level of qualifications necessary to make a correct decision. The structure of the company will help to encourage or discourage decentralization. A flat organization, which has a small number of managerial levels, will encourage it because responsibility will be divided between fewer levels and because managers with a wide span of control will have less time to supervise their subordinates.

Job Description

A subject on which top management in one company may differ vigorously from that in another is the extent to which it is desirable to define the responsibilities of a job ('job description'), and to specify the qualifications necessary to fill the particular job ('job specification'). At one extreme top management might appoint a general sales manager and just leave it to him to sell the product. At the opposite extreme, before looking for a general sales manager, a careful job description may be drawn up of what the job involves and from that a specification made of the kind of man needed to fill it. The illustrative job description given by Brech, an ardent advocate of the value of these descriptions, for such a post lists forty-nine responsibilities which include, for instance:

25. Taking up with the Managing Director, and/or the General Production Manager, any matters which prevent the smooth coordination of Manufacturing and Sales;
41. Providing general supervision of the work of the Export Department to ensure conformity with policy and programme, the maintenance of the Company's standards and reputation, and keeping expenditure within budgeted limits;
48. Encouraging Sales Supervisors, Engineers and Agents to offer constructive suggestions in regard to improvements of the Company's products.[4]

One argument used in favour of the first approach, that is, leaving the scope of the job up to the individual, is that if you appoint a man with initiative he will be able to make his own job and that he should not be hampered or limited by being given precise terms of reference. Another is that in most companies conditions are always changing; therefore, any attempt to define precisely the responsibilities attached to jobs is bound to get rapidly out of date. Those who support the second approach argue that definition of responsibilities is essential if top management is to make certain that no aspect of the work is overlooked because nobody is clearly responsible for doing it; it is also suggested that much personal friction can be avoided if people know exactly what they are responsible for and to whom. The latter argument is based on a very different approach from

4. Brech, E. F. L., op. cit., pp. 144–8.

the belief, which is held by some of those who oppose detailed job descriptions, that if a good man is given a job he will enlarge it, and that if this means he takes over part of somebody else's job this merely does not matter, but may be all to the good as it shows who is the better manager. Before top management appoints the managers in the new company it will have to decide which approach it favours; if it approves of detailed job descriptions it will then need to consider whether conditions are likely to be suitable for them.

Reorganizing a Company

So far we have discussed the organizational decisions which must be made by a top management that is planning a new company. We have done this because it is easier to describe the kind of decisions that have to be made and the sort of problems which will require consideration. Yet the establishment of a new company that is large enough to have a formal-management structure is a comparatively rare event. The reorganization of existing companies is much more common when many of the same considerations will apply. All of them will have to be examined if a really thorough reorganization is being planned. Companies change: the conditions in which they operate may alter, they may expand, change their products, gradually acquire a different type of management, and so on. Any or all of these may be reasons why the existing organization no longer seems satisfactory. Many companies have grown piecemeal often, at least to some extent, around personalities. The posts that were developed by the abilities and weaknesses of particular people may continue after they have left. At some time or other in a company's development, particularly when it is growing past the one-man business stage – which sometimes in practice may not be until it is quite a sizeable company – management will feel a need to re-examine the organization. Then, as in the company that is being planned before it is established, management may ask the question: 'What principles are there in planning an efficient organization?'

and perhaps, even more specifically, 'Is there a best way of organizing a business?'

THE SEARCH FOR PRINCIPLES

In their search for help in planning an organization, management may turn to theorists. The history of theories of organization starts with F. W. Taylor and Henri Fayol, who wrote around the turn of the century. From Fayol onwards, the writers have been preoccupied with defining principles of organization which would be universally applicable. Readers who are interested in a summary of the history of organization thought are referred to the excellent apendix at the back of Brech's book.[5] One trend is the more tentative nature of the principles put forward. In spite of this Brech concludes that:

the contemporary scene shows evidence, too, of growing uniformity of opinion as to what constitutes a 'sound organization'. This means that, unwittingly and implicitly, there is increasing acceptance of an underlying body of 'principles', though it may still be a long time before the practising executive is prepared overtly to admit their existence.[6]

The main writer in this country, who is also recognized as an authority in the USA, is Lyndall Urwick.[7] He has been writing about principles of organization for twenty-five years. We therefore choose to illustrate the thinking of the theorists by giving below his revised list of principles, published in 1952. They are:

1. *The Principle of the Objective*
   Every organization and every part of the organization must be an expression of the purpose of the undertaking concerned or it is meaningless and therefore redundant.
2. *The Principle of Specialization*
   The activities of every member of any organized group

5. op. cit., pp. 363–98.
6. ibid., p. 395.
7. *Notes on the Theory of Organization*, American Management Assoc., New York, 1952.

should be confined, as far as possible, to the performance of a single function.

3. *The Principle of Coordination*
The purpose of organizing *per se*, as distinguished from the purpose of the undertaking, is to facilitate coordination; unity of effort.

4. *The Principle of Authority*
In every organized group the supreme authority must rest somewhere. There should be a clear line of authority from the supreme authority to every individual in the group.

5. *The Principle of Responsibility*
The responsibility of the superior for the acts of his subordinate is absolute.

6. *The Principle of Definition*
The content of each position, both the duties involved, the authority and responsibility contemplated and the relationships with other positions, should be clearly defined in writing and published to all concerned.

7. *The Principle of Correspondence*
In every position the responsibility and the authority should correspond.

8. *The Span of Control*
No person should supervise more than five, or at the most, six, direct subordinates whose work interlocks.

9. *The Principle of Balance*
It is essential that the various units of an organization should be kept in balance.

10. *The Principle of Continuity*
Reorganization is a continuous process; in every undertaking specific provision should be made for it.

How useful are these principles to the managers who are planning a new organization or changing an old one? Most of them offer only very general guidance rather than a blueprint for the design of an organization. Principles 1, 3, and 9 could be used as a starting point for criticisms of an existing organization, but would be of limited help in planning a new one; nor could they offer any guidance on many problems that arise. Of what help, for instance, would the principle of balance be to the managing director who knows that the success of his firm depends above all upon aggressive selling? Principle 2 is more specific, although there is the escape clause, 'as far as possible'; so that, presumably, if you are a smallish firm and have a man who is very good at two dissimilar functions you may create a job for him which is built round his abilities rather than, as in a larger firm, find a man to fit the job. The interpretation of what is a single function may cause difficulties once a firm is large enough for the main functions to be sub-divided.

Principle 10, which is important, merely tells management what must be done but does not – and need not – specify how to do it. Principles 4 and 5 are straightforward and fairly generally accepted. Principle 7 also has wide support, at least in theory, although whether it is upheld in practice will depend on the attitudes of individual managers as well as on official policy. Principle 6 is specific and its validity would be challenged by many, for the reasons given earlier in this chapter. The main objection is that such definition is impractical in any organization which has to adapt itself to rapidly changing conditions.

Since Principle 8, the span of control, is one of the few specific management principles, and one which is widely quoted, it is worth discussing in some detail. Graicunas's mathematical formulation of the principle[8] is based on his idea that there is one main limitation of the number of subordinates who could be effectively supervised. This is that the supervisor must keep in mind not only the direct relationship between himself and each subordinate, but also his relationship with different groupings of the subordinates and the cross relationships between all the subordinates. ('Subordinates' refer only to supervisory and executive personnel.) He calculated that with four subordinates

8. Urwick, Lyndall F. – 'The Manager's Span of Control', *Harvard Business Review*, vol. 34, no. 3, pp. 39–47, May-June 1956 – says that as far as he knows the first person to direct public attention to the principle of the span of control was the late General Sir Ian Hamilton in *The Soul and Body of an Army*, p. 229, Edward Arnold & Company, London, 1921. In 1930, Graicunas developed a mathematical proof of the validity of the principle.

the number of group and cross relationships is 44, but that with six subordinates it increases to 222. Urwick suggests, that because there is a limit to the number of items that the human brain can keep within its grasp simultaneously, it is doubtful if any individual can keep track, and understand the relationships involved, of more than five, or at most six, direct subordinates, and that such understanding is necessary if a man is to lead, not merely administer.[9]

Graicunas noted that where there are few working contacts between the subordinates the relationships will be less complex. This is why Urwick added to his principles the modification 'subordinates whose work interlocks'. He suggests that stores, and departments within one store, may be examples of little interlocking and that hence a much larger number of managers can report to one chief. This could explain the wide span of control in the Sears Roebuck organization, the large American chain store, often quoted as an example of the fallacy of the principle of the span of control.

Brech, who modified the principle to 'a reasonable number', suggested that the following should be considered in deciding what is reasonable: the emotional aspect of attention – that is, the ability of the individual supervisor to deal with interruptions; the amount of time the supervisor has available – when, for instance, the chief executive spends much of his time on public activities, he will have less time to spend with his subordinates; the geographical spread of subordinates; and, finally, the nature and diversity of the responsibilities carried out by the superior and the subordinates.[10]

A number of studies of the span of control in practice shows that it varies widely between companies. The average span of control for senior managers in the companies studied is wider than that given by Urwick and the range is much greater. An American study examined the span of control of the chief executive of 620 manufacturing companies in Ohio with 100 or more employees. (Chief executive also included managers of branch plants.) These companies covered a very wide range of industry. It should be noted that the inquiry was limited to manufacturing companies and therefore excluded large retail stores which may have a wider span of control. This study showed that the average span of control of the chief executive increased as the number of employees went up. In the firms studied that had 1,400 to 3,000 employees the most frequent span was eight subordinates; in firms with over 3,000 employees it was nine. In these larger firms 62.7 per cent of all the main-plant executives had a span of seven or more subordinates. In the plants with less than 1,500 employees the most common spans were four, five or six subordinates. The span of control was also found to vary according to the type of industry. Higher spans were more common in the main plants of paper, and allied products of petroleum and coal; and in branch plants they were more common for stone, clay and glass products, primary metal products, electrical machinery, equipment and supplies, and miscellaneous manufacturing.[11]

Another American study, this time of the number of executives reporting to the chief executive in 100 companies employing over 5,000 people, yielded similar results. All the firms included in this study were described by the American Management Association as having good management practices. The median number of subordinates was between eight and nine and the range from one to twenty-four. The chief executives of 24 firms had thirteen or more subordinates reporting directly to them.[12]

A comparative study of a number of industrial organizations in different European countries suggested further factors that may affect the span of control in practice and make

11. Healey, James H., *Executive Coordination and Control*, Ohio Bureau of Business Research, College of Commerce and Administration, The Ohio State University, 1956.

12. Dale, Ernest, 'Planning and Developing the Company Organization Structure', *Research Report no.* 20, pp. 56–8, American Management Assoc., New York, 1952.

a comparison of the average span of control rather unrealistic.[13] One is the use of staff assistants to relieve the line manager and thus make possible a wider span of control. In practice they may function as an intervening level of management, although this is rarely shown on organization charts. Another factor is the extent and quality of lateral communications; where these are well developed much of the coordination may be done by the subordinates themselves without reference to their manager. This will lighten his load and make possible a wider span of control. The research also showed that the actual span of control is sometimes different from that shown on the organization chart as the manager may encourage people other than his immediate subordinates to discuss problems with him. He may take a particular interest in one function, such as training, although the training officer is shown on the chart several levels below him. A distinction should, therefore, be made between the number of people who are supervised, that is, who report directly to the superior, and the number who have access to him. In particular, access to the chief executive, which can be an important factor in morale, will take up the superior's time and may, therefore, make a small span of direct control 'reasonable'.

These different studies show that the principle of a specific span of control is unrealistic. In practice the formal span of control varies considerably. The burden imposed on a manager by a particular number of subordinates depends on a great variety of factors, including temperamental characteristics such as the extent to which he can be frequently interrupted without becoming upset; questions of ability both of the superior and of his subordinates; the physical location; the nature of the work, including the type and frequency of the decisions which have to be made; and the strength of informal organization. The latter can

13. European Productivity Agency, 'A Study of Post-War Growth in Management Organizations: Comparison of Chemical and Engineering Firms in Eight Western European Countries', *Project no.* 347, pp. 12–14.

reduce the pressure on the manager as subordinates may coordinate much of the work themselves – we shall be looking at the nature and uses of informal organization in the next chapter.

THE SOCIAL SCIENTISTS LOOK AT MANAGEMENT STRUCTURE

We said at the beginning of this chapter that there are two groups of writers on organization. One, the theorists, who produced the traditional theory of organization which is based on the idea of universally applicable principles. The other, the investigators, or social scientists, who seek to find out how organizations work in practice. So far we have described the work of the first group, now we turn to the second.

The approach of most of the theorists tends to be similar, but that of the social scientists is almost bewilderingly varied. As Mason Haire points out, in his symposium on recent research on organization, a parallel would be the fable of the blind men describing an elephant.

There is little doubt here that it is a single elephant being discussed, but, by and large, each of the observers begins his description from a different point, and often with a special end in view. Each of the authors is dealing with organizations and how they work; but, to some extent, they start from different bases and have different things in mind which need explaining.[14]

In looking at organization the social scientists have a much wider range of interest than the traditional management writers. Some start with a study of how organizations work in practice and then try to find out whether their observations can be classified and provide the basis for hypotheses which can then be tested. Some are particularly interested in the human repercussions of certain types of organization. Others make use of game theory, decision theory or information theory, in the construction of models.

14. Haire, Mason (editor), *Modern Organization Theory: A Symposium of the Foundation for Research on Human Behaviour*, p. 2, John Wiley, New York, 1959. (Chapman & Hall, London, 1959.)

One approach to the study of organizations is to look at the functions that have to be performed in particular companies, or departments, and find out how effectively they are being carried out. This kind of research is trying to answer different questions from that which will be described later. It is closest in its interests to the work of the management consultant. An example of this type of research is a study by Professor Herbert Simon and three colleagues which sought 'to expand our knowledge about human behaviour in organizations, and to do this in a way that would cast light on the specific problems of organizing effectively, the controller's department in large companies'.[15] ('Controller' is the American term for the head of the accounting department.) They defined an effective accounting department as one which: provided information of high quality, did so at a minimum cost, and facilitated the long-range development of competent accounting executives. The research workers studied seven large companies which were geographically dispersed. These were in a variety of industries and differed in the extent to which they centralized or decentralized their accounting departments. The research was carried out by interviews, by studying accounting reports and, to a limited extent, by observation.

The research workers found that in each of the companies accounting information was used at various levels to answer three different kinds of questions: one, score-card, 'how am I doing?' two, attention-directing, 'what problems shall I look into?' and three, problem-solving, 'which course of action is better?' The type of information needed varied at different levels of the organization. The extent to which the information was used depended, mainly, on how close was the relationship between the accountants as sources of information and the line people as consumers. To achieve this close relationship different patterns of organization were needed for the different types of information.

15. Simon, Herbert A., Guetzkow, H., Kozmetsky, G., Tyndall, G., *Centralization v. Decentralization in Organizing the Controller's Department*, Controllership Foundation Inc., New York, 1954.

The research showed that there is no such general thing as accounting information. Therefore, in designing the organization of an accounting department one must think of a number of types of data which need different channels of communication if they are to be most useful. As a result of the study the team concluded that there are three major divisions in the accounting function, each of which can be separated from the other. These are record-keeping, current analysis, and special studies for problem-solving purposes. The research workers concluded that:

Combining the functions leads to a potential conflict between the accountant's function, of providing service to operating departments, and his function of analysing operations to provide valid and objective data for higher levels of management. Separating the record-keeping functions from analytical work is also an important supplement to an effective internal audit in reducing the dangers of collusion. It may also give the analytical personnel greater freedom to develop close working relationships with operating executives without a feeling of conflicting responsibilities.

Another reason for separating the functions is to allow greater flexibility for organizing each of them in the most economical and effective manner. ... Each can be centralized or decentralized to the extent that appears desirable, independently of the others.[16]

The above is an example of a study with immediate practical application. It shows how the organization should be designed to meet the needs of those concerned.

Research into organization is still in the early stages. However, there are already a number of pointers which are of potential value to the manager concerned with designing or modifying an organization. One of the most important is that the attempts to deduce principles of organization that were universally applicable may have been misleading. What may be needed is a few general guides to the design, and a number of more detailed blue-prints for different types of business. There should, for instance, probably be

16. ibid., p. 5.

different types of organization for different systems of production.

Peter Drucker in a discussion of principles of production pointed out the following distinctions between unique-product, mass production, and process production:

Under unique-product production, management can be centralized at the top. Coordination between the various functions is needed primarily at the top. Selling, design, engineering, and production, can all be distinct and need only come together where company policy is being determined. It is this pattern of unique-product production that is still largely assumed in our organization theory – even though unique-product production may well be the exception rather than the rule in the majority of American industries today.

Mass production 'old style' can still maintain this pattern, though with considerable difficulty and at a high price in efficiency. It does better with a pattern that establishes centres of decision and integration much further down. For it requires close coordination between the engineers who design the product, the production people who make it, the sales people who market it, and so forth.

In both mass production 'new style' and process production, functional centralization is impossible. They require the closest cooperation of people from all functions at every stage ... And decisions affecting the business as a whole have to be taken at a decentralized level – sometimes at a level not even considered 'management' today.[17]

By mass production 'old style' Drucker means the manufacture of uniform products in large quantity. By mass production 'new style' he means the manufacture of uniform parts which are then mass-assembled into many different products.

Drucker's analysis of the different organizational needs of different production processes is supported by a study by Joan Woodward of the organization of 100 firms in the area of the S.E. Essex Technical College. She tried to find out whether there was a common pattern in the great variety of

17. Drucker, Peter F., *The Practice of Management*, pp. 90–91. Heinemann, London, 1955, and Harper & Bros, New York, 1954.

organizations she discovered. At first she could find none, but when the firms were divided into three groups according to their type of production – mass, batch and single unit, and process – she found that the successful firms in each group had a similar pattern, but one which differed from the successful firms with another system of production. These three patterns were determined, she suggested, by the 'situational demands' which were imposed by the technique of production. She concluded that:

... it was possible to trace a 'cause and effect' relationship between a system of production and its associated organizational pattern and, as a result, to predict what the organizational requirements of a firm are likely to be, given its production system. For example, the following features can be traced to the technology of each system of production: a coordination of functions and centralization of authority in unit production; an extensive specialization and delegation of authority in mass production; and in process industry a specialization between development, marketing and production, combined with integration within each function and the cooperative character of decision-making.[18]

Another illustration of the way in which the situational demands may influence the type of organization comes from a study by Burns and Stalker. They compared companies in the electronics industry, which were going through a rapid change, with a firm producing rayon filament yarn which had become routine production. This comparison suggested that the amount of change affecting the organization influenced the extent of its flexibility. The research workers distinguished two contrasting types of organization: one, they called 'mechanistic', which is suitable for stable conditions; the other, 'organic', which is adapted to changing conditions. The firm making rayon filament yarn was an example of a mechanistic organization, in it each person—

... knew just what he could do in normal circumstances without consulting anyone else; just what point of deviation from the

18. Woodward, Joan, 'Management and Technology,' *Problems of Progress in Industry*, no. 3, p. 37, Department of Scientific and Industrial Research, HMSO, London, 1958.

normal he should regard as the limit of his competence; and just what he should do when this limit was reached – i.e., report to his superior. The whole system was devised to preserve normality and stability. The downward flow of instructions and orders, and the upward flow of reports and requests for such instructions and orders, were precisely and clearly channelled; it had the characteristics of a smoothly working automatic machine. Since everyone knew both his job and its limits, there was little consultation; contacts ran up and down, from subordinate to superior and vice versa, and the great majority of those contacts resulted in the giving of definite orders. The outstanding characteristic of the structure was that it was mechanical and authoritarian. And it worked very well.[19]

In stable conditions, such as those operating in this company, the organization can be treated as a mechanical structure. In it each job has precisely defined rights and duties and technical requirements. The knowledge of the firm's needs and situation is concentrated at the top, thus making possible a hierarchic, authoritarian form of management structure. When the company is operating in conditions of rapid change it must be much more flexible and have, what Burns and Stalker called, an organic system; that is one in which the boundaries of jobs are fluid and there is more consultation and exchange of information than commands. Inter-action between people also takes place laterally as much as vertically. Each of these types of organization suit their different conditions.

What these, and other, research reports indicate is that there is no one ideal form of organization; hence no universally applicable set of principles, except of the most general kind. The organization will vary according to the needs of the company which will depend upon the demands of its situation. The system of production and the rate of change have both been shown to be relevant to the type of organiza-

19. Croome, Honor, 'Human Problems of Innovation' based on a study by Tom Burns and G. M. Stalker, *Problems of Progress in Industry*, no. 5, p. 12, Department of Scientific and Industrial Research, HMSO, London, 1960.

tion that is needed. Further research may show other aspects of the firm's situation, for instance, the market conditions which should influence its pattern of organization. Management, therefore, needs to examine the company's objectives, and the demands of its situation, before designing or changing the pattern of organization.

WHAT IS A GOOD ORGANIZATION?

So far we have made no reference to the question, 'What is a good organization?' In this we have followed the usual practice in writings on organization. Yet the question is obviously important. The theorist is likely to say that an efficient organization is one which is in accord with the traditional principles of organization. The social scientist that it is one which is adapted to the needs of the situation. What is 'good' depends on the value judgements that are made, which may not be explicitly stated. Most managers would say that the best organization is one which encourages efficiency. Disagreements about what is best can come from different ideas on what makes for efficiency, or from different attitudes to people. Unfortunately our knowledge about what makes for efficiency is still limited, so there is plenty of scope for disagreement. One man, for instance, may stress the value of orderliness, another may emphasize the importance of flexibility. Yet another may be preoccupied with the effects of size. Again, attitudes to people will vary and with them, beliefs about what kind of organization encourages people to be efficient. An organization may also, though more rarely, be judged by its effects on people's happiness. Some, perhaps many, managers will modify an organization for humane reasons – to find a niche for Old Bill, for instance – rather than because they believe that doing so will promote efficiency.

It is now time that we left our discussion of the formal structure and turned to the people who will make it work. In the next chapter, therefore, we shall look at the reciprocal relationship between people and the formal organization.

SUMMARY

In this chapter we examined the problems which face the manager in designing a new organization, or modifying an old one; and considered the help he might get from the writers on organization. We outlined the different decisions that have to be made in planning an organization. First came the division of work, which would depend on the objectives of the business. Second was the further sub-division into line or operational, and staff or specialist, jobs: the former have direct responsibility, the latter exist primarily to provide service and advice. The relationship between the two is a perennial problem of organization. It must be based on mutual confidence, but organizational arrangements can help to promote it. The third was the question of how many levels of authority there would be. Management has to decide whether it wants to limit these to the smallest number possible. For the fourth we looked at the usefulness of organization charts and decided that they could be a useful tool, but one which was often abused. The limitations of such charts were stressed. The fifth was one of the most difficult decisions in planning an organization: how much decentralization there should be. This we found would vary at different periods in the company's history, depending in part on the extent to which common policies exist or are desired. The calibre of junior and middle management and the type of decisions to be made were among the other factors which affect how much decentralization there should be. In the sixth, we examined the arguments for and against job descriptions. Their use depends both on management philosophy and on the rapidity of change.

We divided the writers on organization into two groups: the theorists and the investigators. The theorists, mainly managers and consultants, have developed a set of principles which they believe to be universally applicable. These have wide currency and are often taught in management courses. We suggested, however, that most of them are so general that they can only be of very limited usefulness. We looked at one of the specific principles, 'span of control', and found that research threw considerable doubt on its validity in practice. Modified to 'a reasonable span' it could still be of some use in looking at the working of a particular organization; but what is reasonable would vary both with the individual and the organization.

The investigators have mainly looked at how organizations work in practice. Their approach is bewilderingly varied, but some of the findings can already be of value to management. One of the most important is that there is no one ideal form of organization; hence no universally applicable set of principles for its design. Instead the organization must be designed in accordance with its needs, as these are determined by the demands of its situation. We illustrated this finding with: an American study of the work of the accounting department in seven companies; Joan Woodward's study of the organization of a hundred companies; and Burns and Stalker's study of companies undergoing different rates of change.

Our discussion has shown that when management is planning an organization, whether of a company as a whole or of an individual department, it needs to analyse both the objectives of the company and the demands of the situation. It should also examine at intervals whether the organization is meeting the needs of those concerned.

3

People and Organization

SO FAR WE HAVE discussed the organization without the people who will bring it to life, make it work, and give it its distinctive character. Now we need to look at how people may influence the formal structure, as well as how the latter may affect people's behaviour, by the demands it makes on them and the strains it imposes. First, let us look at an organization as seen through the eyes of a newly-recruited manager and then more broadly at the social relations within an organization.

LEARNING THE ROPES

A manager joining a new company would soon put his foot in it if he relied upon the formal organization as his only guide to how the organization worked. The organization chart may embody management's intentions, but this planned structure is run by people and they will have an effect on how it works in practice. The formal organization does not, and cannot, show all the relationships which grow up between people; though in static conditions it will be more likely to do so than in companies which are undergoing rapid organization for cooperating on their work and an awareness and understanding of this is just as, if not more, necessary to the manager than a knowledge of the formal structure.

Because the informal organization plays such an important part in the functioning of any company a manager, who moves from one firm to another and, to a lesser extent, even from one department to another, must take time to learn how it works and, hence, the best ways to achieve what he wants. He must find out, if he is to work effectively and to get on, how the status order differs from that shown on the chart; who takes the lead, and in what circumstances, and who follows. He must also be sensitive to the power politics, to whether management is divided into cliques and, if so, how the cliques are made up and what their relationship is to each other. Then he will need to know whom he must get on his side if he wishes to sell an idea. In one company it will usually be sufficient to get the support of the managing director. In another, subordinates as well as colleagues may need to be in agreement. Again the ways of finding out what is happening in a company will vary. In some there may be committees and meetings at the management level for the exchange of information; in others, the managers' dining-room may be the best source of news. In most companies there will be one or more people who are particularly well-informed about what is happening – 'Ask Old Bill, he will know.' On the shop floor the best place for information may be the lavatory – a useful source for the social research worker but of no use to the manager who will usually be closeted in a separate place.

The new manager will also have to learn the do's and don'ts, the unwritten rules, which may well be different from his previous company. He must learn when, if he wants to know something, he can write or ring and when he must go and see the man. In some companies his acceptance by his colleagues may partly depend on conversation in the managers' dining-room and he should know which topics are barred. Dress may also be subject to some important don'ts – recently in one company when a man asked why he did not get an annual salary increase he was told that it was because he had worn a sweater instead of a jacket which 'showed that he was obviously not taking his management position seriously'. The ambitious manager will want to know what are the standards of taking one's job seriously. In this example, dress was important, elsewhere it may be getting to one's desk early or staying late. But in a few – all too few – companies habitual overtime may be judged a sign of inefficiency. All these informal customs and procedures will help to give an organization its character, will make it different from another company that has the same formal structure. These the new manager must learn before he can become an effective member of the management team. He will benefit from a general understanding of how people work together in an organization, but he will also need the detailed knowledge of how his particular organization works.

SOCIAL RELATIONS AND INFORMAL ORGANIZATION

When people work together they establish social relationships and customary ways of doing things. These cannot be laid down in even the most comprehensive job description as they will depend, at least in part, upon the relations between people – hence, on the kind of people they are, their particular strengths and weaknesses and how they react to each other. Therefore, an organization is not just a collection of isolated individuals performing the specific functions of their allotted jobs. It is also a social system, or a set of social relations, made up of how A reacts to B and both of them to C, of social groups which influence the attitudes and actions of their members and, sometimes, also of a number of cliques or factions – groups that are organized against others. Two things tend to happen when people work together: they may form social groups; and they may develop informal methods of getting their work done, that is, informal organization. Both of these can have important effects on efficiency.

People who work in close contact with each other for any length of time are likely to become a social group. They are then more than a collection of individuals who happen to be working together and they acquire a sense of identity as a group, in which some people are inside and others outside. There may be several social groups within one work group and some individuals who do not belong to a group. The social group is likely to have a sense of like-mindedness among its members and to agree on many subjects of immediate importance to them.

This tendency for people who work together to develop social groups has important implications for management as it can materially assist or considerably handicap management objectives. A number of studies have shown that enthusiasm for work is much greater where group affiliations have been built up, provided the aims of the group do not run counter to those of management. People enjoy their work more, and are less likely to be absent from work, because they have become part of a social group in which they are important as a person. The armed services believe in the value of such groups and use cadres as the foundation for a new unit. These consist of experienced men of all ranks who form the basis but, more important, provide the social groups on which the new organization can be built. They will already, if properly chosen, have a loyalty to military aims and will have developed systems for getting work done.[1]

Informal groups within the formal organization can also work against management aims. Numerous research projects have shown that, even with an incentive scheme, workers will not necessarily aim at the highest output they can achieve. Instead a group of workers may establish their own output norm which may well be considerably less than that which could be maintained by the fastest worker, and even less than that of an average worker. The group may establish quite elaborate procedures for ensuring that this norm is obtained but not exceeded. As well, it may apply various forms of pressure to ensure that no individual exceeds the norm.

Hence the informal group will have its own aims which may support or oppose management aims. It will also have its own sanctions which will differ from those in the formal organization: these will consist of the withdrawal of acceptance and help by the group. The degree to which this is done

1. cf. Dubin, Robert, *The World of Work*, p. 303, Prentice-Hall, Englewood Cliffs, New Jersey, 1958.

will depend upon the heinousness of the infringement of the group's aims. In extreme cases the individual may be sent to Coventry. When the informal group is strong its sanctions are likely to be more compelling on a group member than those of management's, since they are more certain to be applied. Management may not catch a culprit who is violating one of the official rules, but the informal group is much more likely to know if one of its members breaks its social code.

Whether the informal group will work with or against management aims will depend, to some extent, on the type of supervision. Studies by the Institute of Social Research, University of Michigan, show that if foremen involve workers in decision-making the latter are more likely to be management-minded.[2] We shall discuss the effects of different types of supervision in Chapter 8.

We have seen that informal, social groups within the company may organize themselves to help or hinder management aims. As Perrin Stryker said:

the informal organization that pervades every company is so complex that it probably could never be completely charted. But it is this hidden operating structure that gets the work done. Indeed, it is the biggest intangible asset – and usually the touchiest open secret – of any management.[3]

One of its greatest advantages is to facilitate coordination. The self-disciplining and self-checking of the informal group means that far less management time and effort are necessary to ensure that work is being carried out satisfactorily. But as we noted earlier this is only valuable where the group is working to further management aims. Let us now look more closely at the nature of such informal organization.

2. Jacobson, E., 'Foreman and Steward, Representatives of Management and the Unions', *Human Relations Program of the Survey Research Center: First Three Years of Development*, pp. 18–21, Institute of Social Research, University of Michigan, Ann Arbro, Mich., 1950.

3. Stryker, Perrin, and editors of *Fortune*, *A Guide to Modern Management Methods*, p. 108, McGraw-Hill, New York, 1954.

Informal organization exists at all levels in a company. Its functions, at the management level, according to Chester Barnard are:

the communication of intangible facts, opinions, suggestions, suspicions, that cannot pass through formal channels without raising issues calling for decisions, without dissipating dignity and objective authority, and without overloading executive positions; also to minimize excessive cliques of political types arising from too great divergence of interest and views; to promote self-discipline of the group; and to make possible the development of important personal influences in the organization.[4]

Hence informal organization can serve to sift information and ideas before they go to formal authority. Many things, too, can be done informally, often with the knowledge and agreement of senior management, which it would be embarrassing to acknowledge as official policy.

We so often take informal organization for granted that we tend to talk as if it did not exist. Many top managers when asked about the organization of their company would describe the formal organization without adding any reservations about the way it operates in practice. A description of how top management worked in a medium-sized company will illustrate some of the differences between the formal and informal organization. The organization chart showed all the senior managers who reported to the managing director on the same level.[5]

Managing Director

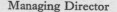

| Works Manager 'A' | Works Manager 'B' | Sales Manager | Company Secretary | Chief Accountant |

4. Barnard, Chester, *The Functions of the Executive*, p. 225, Harvard University Press, Cambridge, Mass., 1958 (originally published Oxford University Press, 1938).

5. The details of this illustration are altered to ensure complete anonymity.

Preliminary inquiries soon revealed that the managing director's subordinates were not all departmental heads of equal importance. The sales manager was really only a junior clerk, since the managing director took a strong personal interest in sales, so that in effect he acted as the sales manager, playing an active part in the day-to-day running of the department. To show the actual position the chart should be redrawn like this:

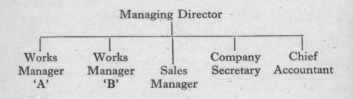

It would not take much time to discover the actual status and responsibility of the sales manager, but it would probably need some experience of how top management worked in practice to find out that one of these senior managers, the chief accountant, was the most important. He was frequently consulted by the managing director on many aspects of the business and was also used by his colleagues, because his advice carried weight with the managing director, to interpret their grievances or their ideas to him. The role of the chief accountant in helping top management to run smoothly was thus discovered to be an important factor in the informal organization of top management, but one that could not have been guessed at by looking at the organization chart.

The redrawn organization chart suggested that not only were the four managers, still shown on the same level, of equal importance, but also that each would always deal directly with the managing director when he wanted his agreement to a new project. A more realistic picture of what happened in practice in this company might be shown in a chart which looked like this:

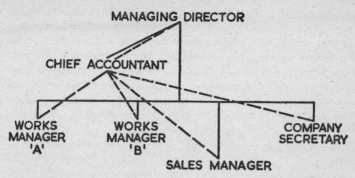

The dotted lines show the second channel for communication. The chief accountant is not put in a direct line between the managing director and the other top managers as he does not function, either officially or unofficially, as the assistant managing director, but merely as adviser and interpreter.

Chester Barnard, discussing a similar role to that of the chief accountant's, suggested that:

... many men not only exercise beneficent influence far beyond that implied by their formal status, but most of them, at the time, would lose their influence if they had corresponding formal status. The reason may be that men may have personal qualifications of high order that will not operate under the stress of commensurate official responsibility.[6]

Such a man can help to reduce the isolation of the chief executive, by acting as a trusted go-between who carries messages to and from the heights. In the example given above, top management worked more efficiently because the role played by the chief accountant helped to offset the managing director's weaknesses in dealing with his subordinates. The success of the chief accountant's role was, however, based on trust; the other top managers found that it was easier to get the managing director to listen to what

6. op. cit., p. 226.

they wanted if they could persuade the chief accountant to sell their ideas or explain their grievances for them, and they trusted him to put them forward in good faith. The managing director also trusted the advice of the chief accountant. Such a relationship can only work harmoniously where there is an absence of personal animosity. (In the company from which we draw our example this was helped by the fact that it was a family firm and the managing director would be succeeded by his son, so that the other managers could not compete for promotion to the managing director's chair.) Where there are personality clashes an informal organization based on cliques may develop, which is harmful to efficiency. If, for instance, the other managers had not trusted the chief accountant, they would have resented his close relations with the managing director and might have banded together and given him only the minimum cooperation.

Informal organization may also develop to by-pass or protect an inefficient individual or group. In one company, for instance, as other departments found that the sales control department was inaccurate and behind in its work, they gradually took to doing the work themselves, but routing the final estimates through the sales department. Senior management was unaware of what was happening and nobody would tell them for fear of getting their colleagues in sales control into trouble. In this example good relations masked inefficiency. This may often happen when colleagues seek to cover up the slowness or inefficiency of one of their number. Such 'covering up' need not necessarily stem from antagonism to management. Sometimes, of course, it does, especially on the shop floor.

Informal organization, as we have seen, modifies the formal structure. It may be developed to combat management aims – when a group of workers will restrict output. But it may also be developed by people to adjust the formal organization to the needs of the situation. Then it can be most useful. It may grow up primarily for personality reasons as in the two examples above. Informal organization adjusts to the strengths and weaknesses of people; by so doing it can increase efficiency. In the example of top management organization, the role of the chief accountant greatly improved communication between the managing director and the other top managers; if the managing director had been a different kind of person he would have dealt direct with his managers more often. At lower levels difficult or inefficient people, who hamper the normal functioning of the formal organization, will cause others to try to by-pass them, often if they are inefficient but likeable, to cover up for them.

Informal organization may also grow up because rapid change makes the formal organization out-of-date. Initially, in changing conditions people will try to solve problems on an *ad hoc* basis as they arise but, sooner or later, if formal organization is not adapted to meet the new situation, they will develop informal organization to help it. If, for instance, inter-departmental meetings are not set up to keep people in the picture, managers from different departments may make a habit of dropping in to a local pub once or twice a week to try, as one manager put it, 'to sort out the chaos'. The tendency of people to develop informal organization to help their work has probably saved many companies, which have been slow to adapt their formal structure, from some of the worse difficulties that could follow a radical departure from previous activities.

HOW THE ORGANIZATION AFFECTS PEOPLE

So far we have looked at some of the ways in which people may modify the formal organization, but it is a reciprocal influence, for the organization also affects the behaviour of individuals and groups. It can impose pressures on people in particular jobs which may lead them to adopt informal means of trying to avoid, or lessen, the problems of their position. The influence of the organization on the behaviour of individuals is most clearly seen when people in the same jobs in different parts of the organization are found to react in similar ways. A study by Ralph H. Turner[7] showed the pressures on the disbursement officer in the American Navy (supply officer), which were such that in trying to adjust to them the officer was likely to distort official regulations. The particular problems of the disbursement officer's job were: one, possible conflicts between regulations governing his function and orders from his superior, both of which were supposed to be obeyed; two, the fact that he held a lower rank than that of many of his clients; three, pressure from people with whom he was in close contact and who wanted him to interpret the regulations in their favour. The last was made more difficult by a well-developed informal system for the exchange of favours, so that it was often hard for a man to get the services and equipment essential for his job, quite apart from personal goods, unless he could promise some return. If the disbursement officer stuck to the strictly formal procedure he lost his potentially strong position in the system of mutual benefits. According to Ralph Turner:

Two general tendencies emerge among disbursing officers as the consequences of orders conflicting with regulations and the pressures of rank and informal structure. One is differential treatment of clientele. Because of the time consumed in extra-routine treatment of persons on the 'in', others get summary treatment. The second tendency is for loop-holes in regulations to become tools in the hand of the disbursing officer to elevate his own status. Thus he may become more concerned with his own bargaining power than with correct application of rules.[8]

Another illustration of the way in which people, subject to the same organizational pressures, may react in the same way comes from a study of the relations between production and inspection. This is a potentially difficult relationship because of the criticism inherent in inspection. Messrs McKenzie and Pugh, who studied the relations between the two in a number of factories, found that where the two activities were organizationally separate there tended to be

7. 'The Navy Disbursing Officer as a Bureaucrat', *American Sociological Review*, pp. 342–8, vol. 12, June 1947.

8. ibid., pp. 347–8.

a consistent pattern of comments at all levels in production. All would query the inspector's technical knowledge, complain that an important job was stopped, say that the criticized dimensions were irrelevant to the product's ultimate function and that, in general, the inspector did not understand production difficulties. The authors suggest that if 'the relation between inspection and production is organized in a given way, then certain pressures will occur and certain attitudes, comments and complaints will appear'.[9]

These, and other studies, show that many reactions which are put down to individual cussedness are due to pressures imposed by the situation in which the person has to work. Pressures that are likely to produce a similar reaction in people of very different personalities. These are important findings for they show that managers need to think more of the strains which may result from the organization. Problems are usually discussed in terms of personality, but the remedy may be to change the organization rather than the people. Several studies also show that the nature of the technological organization can have important effects on the social relations in the working group. It can, for instance, determine the amount and type of social contact that people can have with one another, hence the likelihood of social groups and satisfying relations developing. (Though, as we shall see in Chapter 10, there is some choice in the methods of organizing work so as to make such satisfying relations possible.)

A study by Walker and Guest of assembly line workers in a car factory showed that the technological layout and the high noise level, imposed considerable restrictions on the amount of contact workers could have with one another. It also largely determined the amount and type of contact they had with supervision.[10] A study by the Tavistock Institute of

9. McKenzie, R. M., and Pugh, D. S., 'Some Human Aspects of Inspection', *The Institution of Production Engineers Journal*, vol. 36, no. 6, pp. 378–87, June 1957.

10. Walker, Charles R., and Guest, Robert H., *The Foreman on the Assembly Line*, Harvard University Press, Cambridge, Mass., 1952.

Human Relations of different methods of coal-getting showed that a change in the method had radically altered the kind of social relationships which had developed in association with the old method.[11] In another report by the Tavistock Institute of Human Relations on different methods of coal-getting, the research workers found striking differences between output, costs, and absenteeism for two methods of work organization. For instance, the absenteeism rate from all causes was 20 per cent of possible shifts under one method and 8.2 per cent under another.[12]

The authors of these studies thought that some of the problems of management-worker relations stemmed from the fact that the method of work organization prevented the worker from establishing satisfactory social relations. We saw earlier in this chapter that the growth of social groups could be of value to morale, since people then tended to enjoy their work more. It seems from these studies that to organize work so that pleasant social relations have no opportunity to develop is likely to be bad for morale.

Professor Argyris, a well-known American writer on industrial relations, has attacked the traditional shop-floor organization for the demands it makes on the worker. He suggests that informal organization for restriction of output is a result of an inherent conflict between the demands of the formal organization and the needs of a psychologically healthy individual.[13] He argues that formal organization based on principles of task specialization, unity of direction, chain of command and span of control, demands that the worker shall be dependent, subordinate and passive towards the leader. This will make a psychologically healthy person – by that Argyris primarily means mature – feel

11. Trist, E. L., and Bamforth, K. W., 'Some Social and Psychological Consequences of the Longwall Method of Coal-Getting', *Human Relations*, vol. 4, no. 1, pp. 3–38, 1951.

12. Emery, F. E., and Trist, E. L., 'Socio-Technical Systems', *Management Sciences: Models and Techniques*, vol. 11, p. 81, Pergamon Press, London, 1960.

13. Argyris, Chris, *Personality and Organization: The Conflict Between System and Individual*, Harper Bros, New York, 1957.

failure, frustration and conflict. He will also develop a short-term view, whereas a mature person looks further ahead.

The worker may seek to adjust himself to the conflict between his needs to be active, creative, and independent and the demands of the organization by leaving the company, or by working hard to climb the ladder to a position where conditions are less frustrating. One of the other ways by which he may adjust is by becoming apathetic and aggressive. This will show itself in a loss of interest in work and in a desire to 'get even' with management. It results in restriction of output, slowing-down and goldbricking; that is, secretly stock-piling finished work so that the worker may have as much time as possible in which to do what he likes. Informal work groups, according to Argyris, are organized to sanction and perpetuate these methods of adaptation. Restriction of output is widespread. It is important to try to understand the reasons. England, according to J. A. C. Brown, could increase her national income by one-half within five years if employee apathy was decreased.[14] So far efforts to do so have concentrated on increasing incentives, but the studies we have just quoted suggest another approach, that of organizing work so that it is socially satisfying. In the chapter on 'Getting the Job Done' we shall examine in greater detail the different attempts to increase the worker's willingness to work.

SUMMARY

This chapter has looked at the influence of people on the formal organization. We have seen how the structure may be modified by the people who make it work, so that even identical organizations will develop their own distinctive characters. The informal organization that grows up can be a great asset, as it can make allowances for personalities, adapt to change and facilitate coordination. The social groups which tend to develop among those working closely together may also be an important factor in promoting

14. Brown, J. A. C., *The Social Psychology of Industry*, p. 87, Penguin Books, Harmondsworth, Middx., 1954.

good morale, because people will then find their work more socially satisfying. We saw, however, that the social groups may also work against management aims; for instance, when a group of workers develops its own informal organization to restrict output.

We found that the relationship between organization and people is a reciprocal one. People modify the working of the formal organization, but their behaviour is also influenced by the organization. It may make demands on them, which they find an undue strain, so that they seek ways of modifying these pressures. We saw, too, that the method of work organization can determine what kind of relationships people have with one another, and that this may affect both their productivity and morale. Management, therefore, needs to be conscious of the ways in which methods of work organization may influence people's attitudes and action. Before behaviour is put down to individual or group cussedness, management should look for its possible organizational causes.

PART TWO
The Job

This section has four chapters. The first looks at the theoretical writing on the manager's functions; then at what is known – all too little – about how managers work in practice. The manager's job is divided into making decisions and getting the job done. Each of these is discussed in a separate chapter, with examples from research which should help the manager to make better decisions and to implement them more successfully. The last chapter summarizes what research on leadership can tell us about the nature of the manager's job, and its relevance to the selection and development of managers. The first three chapters look at the manager's job in general. The fourth shows how his functions as a leader will vary according to the situation and its problems.

4

What Does the Manager Do?

IN PART ONE we looked at the organization within which the manager has to work. Now we turn to the manager himself, to find out what is known about the nature of his job, and about selecting and training the right kind of managers. We shall also look at some of the problems inherent in his work. What is the manager's job? To ask this question implies that there is *a* management job; that there are common elements in any management job, whether it is that of a works manager in a small firm in the light-engineering industry, a sales manager in a medium-sized company selling canned fruit, or the chief accountant of a large firm in the steel industry. Is it possible to separate and define these elements? The first part of this chapter summarizes what is generally accepted as the manager's functions. The second part looks at what we know about the manager's job in practice.

THE MANAGER'S JOB: THEORY

Functions

For over fifty years, from Henri Fayol in 1908 to the present day, the management theorists have been analysing the nature of the manager's job so that they can generalize about his functions. Some of the writers use different words to mean the same thing, but if allowance is made for this there is broad agreement about the manager's functions. First, he must plan: set objectives, forecast, analyse problems, and make decisions – that is, formulate policy. (Some writers, however, say that 'setting objectives' is the function of the directors. In the broadest sense this is, or should be, true.) Secondly, the manager organizes: he determines what activities are necessary to achieve the objectives, he classifies the work, divides it and assigns it to groups and individuals. Thirdly, a manager motivates: that is, he inspires his staff to contribute to the purposes of the organization, to be loyal to its aims and to pull their weight in achieving them. Drucker groups motivation with communication – one of the means that must be used in influencing people to work well. He describes concisely what is involved in this aspect of the manager's job:

Next a manager motivates and communicates. He makes a team out of the people that are responsible for various jobs. He does that through the practices with which he manages. He does it in his own relation to the men he manages . . . He does it through constant communication, both from the manager to his subordinate, and from the subordinate to the manager.[1]

Fourthly, the manager controls what is done by checking performance against the plans. Drucker uses the word 'measurement' instead of 'control'.[1] This is not just a synonym for it suggests a shift in emphasis from seeing that orders are obeyed, to setting objectives and providing the yardsticks for self-control. The idea of control as something imposed upon one's subordinates is replaced by the idea of guidance and the establishment of standards.

To these four functions, planning, organizing, motivating, and controlling, some authors, including Brech and Urwick, add coordinating. But this seems to be too general a term to be satisfactorily isolated as *an* element in the manager's job. Coordination involves planning, as in the division of duties between jobs; it also involves communication if it is to be effective, as well as motivation and control. As Sune Carlson, a Swedish professor of business administration, has pointed out, 'The concept of coordination does not describe a *particular set* of operations but *all* operations which lead to a certain result, "unity of action".[2]

1. Drucker, op. cit., p. 303.
2. Carlson, Sune, *Executive Behaviour: A Study of the Work Load and the Working Methods of Managing Directors*, p. 24, Strombergs, Stockholm, 1951.

Drucker makes an important addition to the four functions that, although sometimes under different names, are described by the main theorists; it is the development of people. He attaches so much importance to this that he says:

... the function which distinguishes the manager above all others is his educational one. The one contribution he is uniquely expected to make is to give others vision and ability to perform.[3]

He stresses that, though the manager may not think of the development of people as part of his job, by the way he manages:

he makes it easy or difficult for them to develop themselves. He directs people or misdirects them. He brings out what is in them or he stifles them. He strengthens their integrity or he corrupts them. He trains them to stand upright and strong or he deforms them.[4]

Definitions

The definitions of management are more varied than the descriptions of its functions. Brech defines management as:

A social process entailing responsibility for the effective (or efficient) planning and regulation of the operations of an enterprise, such responsibility involving – (a) the installation and maintenance of proper procedures to ensure adherence to plans and (b) the guidance, integration and supervision of the personnel comprising the enterprise and carrying out its operations.

or more simply as:

Planning and regulating (or guiding) the activities of an enterprise in relation to its procedures, and to the duties or tasks of its personnel.[5]

Barnard, in his well-known book, *The Functions of the Executive*, stresses that:

3. Drucker, op. cit., p. 309.
4. ibid., p. 304.
5. Brech, E. F. L., *Management: Its Nature and Significance*, p. 30, Pitman London, third edition, 1953.

Executive work is not that *of* the organization, but the special-ized work of *maintaining* the organization in operation.[6]

Sir Charles Renold, in one of the most widely quoted definitions in Britain, said that:

Management is the process of getting things done through the agency of a community.[7]

He distinguished between the things to be done, the purpose, on the one hand, and the well-being of the community through which the purpose is pursued on the other. He then extended his definition to:

the functions of management are the handling of a community with a view to its fulfilling the purposes for which it exists.[8]

Drucker describes management as 'a multi-purpose organ that manages a business and manages managers and man-ages workers and work'[9] These three main jobs of manage-ment must all be carried out within an additional dimension, that of time, since management must think of both the present and the future. Drucker's description of manage-ment is different in nature from the others we have quoted as he is concerned with what has to be done rather than with how it has to be done. It is a helpful description because it is more concrete than the others and pinpoints different aspects of the manager's job.

All these definitions can be useful in thinking about the nature of the manager's job. But we want a simple definition that can be used when we discuss the manager's job in prac-tice in subsequent chapters. A distinction can be made in the manager's functions between *deciding what to do* and *getting it done*. The manager's job can, therefore, be broadly defined as 'deciding what should be done and then getting other people to do it'. A longer definition would be concerned with how these two tasks are to be accomplished.

6. Barnard, Chester, op. cit., p. 215.
7. 'The Nature of Management', *Occasional Papers No. 2*, p. 4, British Institute of Management, London, 1949.
8. ibid., p. 14.
9. op. cit., p. 13.

The first task involves setting objectives, planning, including decision-making, and setting up formal organization. The second consists of motivation, communication, control including measurement, and the development of people. The two tasks are separated for convenient analysis, but in practice they may often overlap. For instance, a manager who wishes to reach a decision acceptable to his subordinates, and therefore more easily implemented, may involve them in the process of decision-making.

It is not necessary to consider here which policy decisions are made by the Board and which by management. Practice varies from one company to another. It is sufficient for our discussion of the manager's job that all managers must be concerned, to some extent, with policy-making.

THE MANAGER'S JOB: PRACTICE

We have seen that the theorists are in broad agreement about the content of the manager's job, but their analysis of his functions are extremely general. What is the practical value of these analyses? They should, if they are to be useful, be able to help us with the selection and the training of managers. To a limited extent they can do so. To know, for instance, that managers plan and motivate, can help us to eliminate some people: 'He would never make a manager because he is too muddle-minded ever to be able to plan anything' or 'He is too retiring to be able to motivate anybody'. But the usefulness of such analysis is limited because the job of the manager is so varied: the differences may be as, if not more, important than the similarities. These lists of management functions ignore the diversity of management: that the job of a top manager bears little resemblance to that of a junior manager, or that being a coke-ovens manager in a steel mill is hardly comparable with being an advertising manager to a popular shoe manufacturer. These jobs differ, partly because they have different functions, but even more because the situations of the firms are so dissimilar.

In Part Three we shall consider the firm's situation. We shall see that the manager's job is vitally affected by it. If he works in a process industry his job will be different from the same post in a mass production industry. If he belongs to a company that is struggling in a highly competitive industry, his job may have little similarity to that of a manager in a company which merely has to maintain its good name in a near-monopoly position. Again managing in a large company has important differences from managing in a small one; for instance, both the amount of specialization and the type of contact with staff will vary. Above all, as we shall see in the last chapter, the rate of change can transform the nature of the manager's job. The theorists have concentrated on the similarities in the manager's job, but the research that we shall describe in later chapters, highlights the importance of the differences. No adequate section and training can take place unless these differences are appreciated. 'A good manager can manage anything' is a common statement. Its truth is attested to by some of our leading managers. Yet it is a belief that is rarely put into practice in industry. Changes between functions in the same company are infrequent and restricted. Moves between companies are rare: most managers who tried to change their company will know what a heart-breaking attempt it can be. Two reasons are usually given for this immobility: one, the amount of technical knowledge required, particularly at the lower levels and two, the need to know one's way round in the company. We saw in the last chapter that learning the ropes was an essential part of the new manager's job. Most companies are unwilling to pay a man over the age of 30 while he acquires this knowledge. In general, therefore, management does not behave as if it believes that a good man can manage anything.

The statement about good managers comes nearest to the truth at top management level, where the technical content is lowest and where the tone is set by the managing director. Even at top management level, however, the kind of people who have to be managed and the type of problem that has to be resolved can be so diverse that they require different abilities, therefore, different people. The research discussed in the chapter on leadership confirms the need for different types of leaders for different situations. The diversity of the manager's job reduces the value of generalizations about his functions. Another snag is that we know so little about what managers actually do, hence the generalizations are not the end result of research into how managers work. So far the gap between the general statement 'all managers plan, organize, motivate and control', and the detailed description of what they do, has only the flimsiest of trial bridges across it. The theorist's description of the manager's functions is so general that it could apply to any leader anywhere. What we need are more specific descriptions that can be used in management selection and training. The present job descriptions are of restricted use in selection and of little or no help in management development.

We do know, both from common observation and from several research studies,[10] that the way in which managers do their job varies. Some of their activities are determined by the particular post they occupy, but within these limitations managers will tend to spend more time on the work they enjoy and less on the rest. The nature of the job will therefore vary, to some extent, according to the abilities, likes and dislikes of its holders. In one study the greatest variations appeared to be in the amount of time spent in public relations and in direct supervision of subordinates. This is not surprising, as one would expect personality differences to show up most clearly in relations with other people. Some managers, for instance, may get great satisfaction out of performing on a larger stage than their own company and, therefore, make the most out of the opportunities that public relations gives them to do so. Other managers may get their main satisfaction out of close personal contact with their

10. cf. Shartle, C. L., 'Leadership and Executive Performance', *Personnel*, vol. XXV, no. 5, pp. 375–6, 1949. Quoted by Shartle, Carroll L., in *Executive Performance and Leadership*, pp. 88–94, Staples Press, London, 1957.

subordinates. The work pattern of the manager will influence the jobs of his subordinates. A manager who spends a lot of time on public relations will leave some other aspects of his job to be done by his subordinates. As we shall see in the chapter on 'Leadership and Development', these differences in work pattern are important in the selection of a well-balanced team.

A detailed study of what managers do in practice was made shortly after the last war by Sune Carlson,[11] on the work load and working methods of managing directors. This study, the most ambitious that has been carried out, was limited to nine managing directors, and to an analysis of how they spent their time for four weeks. Carlson tried to collect information for every executive action of these nine men in terms of: (1) the place of work; (2) the amount of time spent with other people, and who these people were; (3) the methods of communication, e.g., whether they were direct contacts by conferences, telephone calls, etc., or indirect contacts via staff assistants, etc., or via papers; (4) the nature of the questions handled, classified by field of activity, whether they were questions of development or of current operation, and whether they were concerned with policy or application; (5) the kind of action classified under such headings as getting information, taking decisions, giving orders, inspecting and reviewing.

But a study of nine managing directors in Swedish firms can tell us little, if anything, about the work load or working methods of other top executives in Sweden, still less about those in Great Britain or the USA. It can, however, suggest what Carlson calls administrative pathologies, that is, deviations from what the people concerned consider to be efficient procedures. Carlson found, for instance, that the chief executives he studied were rarely alone and undisturbed in their offices for periods of more than about ten minutes at a time. He also found that they tended to regard their outside activities, which took up to half their time, as a temporary burden, and hence not to plan their work to allow

11. op. cit.

for these activities. It is probable that both of these findings are also true of some British top managers.

An interesting sidelight on possible national differences in working methods is given in Carlson's small comparison of the use of letters as a means of communication. He found that his Swedish subjects wrote a few letters. Some signed not more than two or three a wcck, and the maximum was two or three a day. But he quotes a study of twelve German executives who spent on average two hours a day dictating and thirty minutes a day signing letters.[12] The numbers are, of course, too small to draw any conclusions, but the possible differences are intriguing. Comparisons of the frequency and length of telephone calls and meetings might also show differences, but an extensive study would be necessary before one could know whether such differences are national ones, or due to other factors such as differences in the type of industry or the rate of change.

SUMMARY

In the first half of this chapter we considered the writings on the nature of the manager's job and found that, although terminology differs, there is broad agreement that a manager plans, organizes, controls and motivates. To these Drucker added the 'development of people'. There is disagreement about whether 'coordination' is *a* function of management or a general term for *the* function of a manager. We decided upon a simple definition of management: 'deciding what should be done and then getting other people to do it.' Both of these involve organization which we discussed in Part One. In the rest of Part Two we shall look at the two halves of the manager's job – decision-making and implementation – and, then, at what we know about leadership and how to develop good managers.

So much for theory. When we turned to what is known about the manager's work in practice, we were disappointed. Little is known about what managers actually do or how they do it. We quoted Sune Carlson's pioneering study of

12. ibid., p. 83.

nine managing directors and some research on differences in work patterns that showed how managers varied in the amount of time they spent on different aspects of their jobs. We suggested that the nature of the manager's job may be influenced by its function, its level and by the situation of the firm. Indeed, managers' jobs vary so much that we were doubtful of the truth of the common statement 'a good manager can manage anything'. We decided that the management theorists had over-emphasized the similarities of the manager's job at the expense of the differences which are many and important. They could talk about *the* manager's job because their description of his functions was so general as to be universally valid: but such a level of generalization has a very limited usefulness in practice. In Part Three we shall explore the nature of some of the differences between managers' jobs and their significance. But now we shall look at what is involved in decision-making.

5

Making Decisions

DECISION-MAKING IN industry is now a popular subject for discussion and research. Recognizing that the wrong decision may cost thousands, sometimes even millions of pounds, top management is searching for ways of improving its score of bull's-eyes. Nor need it look far for people who are keen to help – by programming decisions on computers, by using operational research as a means of discovering the best answer to certain types of problems, and by training junior and middle management in decision-taking by the use of business games. Decision-making, like organization, has recently attracted a crowd of research workers from different disciplines. These look at the problems of making decisions from their own points of view and make their own contributions to our still limited knowledge of the subject. It would take too long to try to summarize here all these different and, at present, still sometimes highly theoretical approaches to theories of decision-making. Instead we shall discuss some of the simpler things which are now known about the process of decision-making in practice.

SETTING THE SIGHTS

Decision-making in industry is made simpler if management sets the boundaries within which the business is to operate. These boundaries are established by defining the objectives which should be generally understood whether implicitly or, preferably, explicitly. Writing them down can help to clarify them still further. One of the values of so defining objectives is that it will distinguish them from management beliefs which may be shown to have no present purpose. Out-dated beliefs tend to continue in any organization. In the armed services it used to be known as 'Generals always fight the last war', but it is just as true in business. Managers, for instance, have worried about maximizing production long after the sellers' market has passed and the emphasis should have shifted to quality and price.

Management beliefs and attitudes are likely to have an important influence on both the type of decision that is made and the speed with which a decision is reached and implemented. Some decisions may never be made because they are not in accord with management's beliefs about priorities. Others may not be implemented, or their implementation long delayed, because management, although it gives lip service to the importance of doing so, does not really believe in its value. An example of this, which is all too frequent, is the delay in implementing plans for the development of future managers. If the objectives are clearly defined it will help to reduce, though, probably not wholly to eliminate, the influence of management beliefs which are not in accordance with them.

The objectives may include the kind of products to be manufactured; the type of market to be aimed at; the ethics governing the relations with customers, employees, and the community; and the rate of profit to be sought. Less frequently they may also include other factors such as the location of the plant(s), the desirable size of the company, or an approximate yield on the company's shares in relation to the market average which may be aimed at as an indication of market prestige. The nature of each of these objectives will vary in different companies. One company will aim at the maximum profit although, as Robert A. Gordon has pointed out, the managers of large organizations, in contrast to owner-managers, may place other goals ahead of maximum profits – such as the continuity of the organization, its growth and, hence, their own prestige, or specially good treatment of employees.[1] Another may set a precise profit goal, such as a 10 per cent return on capital.

1. *Business Leadership in the Large Corporation*, pp. 326–335. The Brookings Institution, Washington, D.C., 1945.

A company may set very specific objectives for the type of product to be manufactured and the markets to be aimed at, for instance, making high quality shoes. Such specific objectives are more likely to be found in small and medium-sized companies and in bigger companies in the capital goods industries. In a large and diverse group of companies the product and market objectives may be very general, such as keeping in the consumer-goods industries, or there may even be no limitation on the type of goods to be manufactured. A company which has no product objectives to guide its growth – usually where it is expanded by the acquisition of other firms – must establish other objectives, such as a test of profitability.

The attitude to expansion is an important factor affecting the types of decisions which are made. Most companies aim at expansion; some will only seek it through internal growth, others will also seek to expand by acquisition. The objective of some firms, especially small and medium-sized private businesses, may only be to hold their present market position. Such an objective may be due to lack of capital, to a desire on the part of the owner to maintain sole control, or to his view of what is the optimum size for his business. On ethical objectives, some companies say they have a fourfold responsibility to shareholders, customers, employees and the community. Within this general objective, more specific ones may be set, such as not paying wages which are below the market rate, always replacing faulty products, or, as far as possible, not despoiling the countryside. Some companies vary in the strictness of their ethical objectives between employees and customers with the community often a long way behind. They may justify such differences in standards by saying that the customers can look after themselves, but that employees are less able to do so.

Drucker in the *Practice of Management* attaches great importance to the formulation of objectives.[2] He lists eight areas in which he thinks objectives of performance and results should be set: market standing, innovation,

2. op. cit., p. 53.

productivity, physical and financial resources, profitability, manager performance and development, worker performance and attitude and public responsibility. Few British companies, and probably not many American, define their objectives over so wide a range to include both tangibles and intangibles. The Glacier Metal Company has a very detailed written Company Policy Document which is notable for its attention to relations between members of the organization and the promotion of the well-being of each member.[3] This document includes the following statement of company objectives:

C. *Achievement of the Purpose of the Company*

C. 1. The purpose of the members employed by the Company is the continuity of a working community, the conditions of which will promote the physical and mental well-being of members and, taking into account all possible circumstances, will provide them with the highest possible return for work done. The purpose of the members in this respect is consistent with the legal purpose of the Company as set out in the Memorandum of Association dated the 6th December, 1935, in that both will be achieved by:

C1.1 Ensuring that the Company is able to maintain a high position in the competitive market by reason of its standards of price, quality and service to customers. This involves research, development and achievement of high technical and organizational efficiency.

C.1.2 Providing such dividends for its shareholders as will represent a reasonable and fair return for their capital investment.

C.1.3 Ensuring that every member is paid at a level consistent with the role into which he contracted, and that he gets a level of work consistent with his capacity, if such work is available.

C.1.4 Providing reserves sufficient to safeguard the Company and all who work within it.

C.1.5 Providing the maximum practicable facilities for the

3. Brown, Wilfred, 'Company Policy Document', *Explorations in Management*, Appendix 11. Heinemann, London, 1960.

health, safety and well-being of all members employed by the Company.

RECOGNIZING THE LIMITATIONS

The objectives are the boundaries that management sets on its freedom of decision. They establish the kind of things that management can do and those that are outside its objectives. There are also other limitations on the freedom to make decisions, but these are not self-imposed, although, in an indirect way, they may be the result of previous decisions. The first of these limitations is shortages of money, men, and materials, therefore, many business decisions will mirror the economist's definition of 'the application of scarce means to alternative ends'. One of the advantages of large-scale organization is that it is less limited by shortages of money or men. The second, and often stringent, limitation on managers' freedom of decision is that imposed by outside agencies such as the government or trade unions. A third limitation comes from people's attitudes which we shall be discussing at length in the next chapter on 'Getting the Job Done'. The opposition of individual managers may mean that a decision is never reached or, if it is, the project may founder through lack of support. For instance, the support of the general sales manager for a proposed new product is probably essential to the success of the sales campaign. The opposition of the rank and file may also mean that the decision can never be successfully implemented. The nature and strength of such opposition must be taken into account before a decision is reached.

The kind of limitations imposed on management's freedom of action vary from one company to another and from one country to another. This is true for both economic and social restrictions. The latter will be largely determined, as we shall see in a later chapter, by the social climate prevailing in the country at the time which prescribes what is acceptable behaviour. The particular locality and industry will also have its own traditions, so will the company itself. All these will impose limitations on management's freedom of decision.

ANALYSING DECISION-MAKING

The ways in which decisions are made vary from one company to another. In one, nearly all important decisions are made by a group of managers; in another, the individual manager will often decide on his own. The difference between these two methods is greatest at the top. In one company there will be an active top management committee which takes the major decisions; in another the managing director will take most of these decisions on his own, possibly after consulting his staff. The decision may, or may not, be based on an agreed document or recorded in any form. In some companies there may never be a formal decision, but an understanding on which instructions are based. The latter, like the bare recording of a decision, may later lead to confusion about exactly what was agreed.

In looking at decision-making it is helpful to trace a logical sequence as a guide to the steps which should be carried out in reaching a decision. Before any decision is made, three things should be done. In simple decisions these stages may be passed through very quickly. First, the reasons for taking a decision must be formulated. This can be done by defining a problem that is to be solved. At this stage it is vital to ask the right questions, otherwise the decision may be the right answer to the wrong question. Second, the nature of the problem must be analysed. Third, the alternative solutions must be examined, together with their possible consequences. The correctness of these preliminary stages will have a great influence on the validity of the final decision.

How these steps should be carried out, and what effect they can have on the correctness of the final decision, may be illustrated by an examination of a question which many companies have to consider at some time, 'whether to produce a new product and, if so, which new product?' This, like most decisions in business, is not a single decision. Usually, there are a group of related decisions, or one major decision which entails many subsidiary ones, in addition to the decisions which have to be made at lower levels during implementation. If top management is considering the launching of a new product, the first step is to analyse why it wants to do so. The analysis may show, for instance, one or more of the following: that a competitor recently launched a new product which is capturing some of the market; that the company has surplus production capacity; that the sales force is underemployed at some time of the year or that they want to expand and, or, to diversify. One or more of these may be the reasons why management wants to introduce a new product. The definition of the problem may show that what is required is not a new product but, say, a more intense selling campaign for existing products. We shall assume, however, that the definition of the problem shows that a new product is required. We now pass to the second stage, analysing the nature of the problem, which tells us the kind of new product that is required. The analysis indicates that the new product must meet two needs: diversification, and the full utilization of a selling force that at present sells one seasonal product. Therefore, the new product must have a different sales peak from that of the present one.

The first and second stages are now complete; a new product is required which will meet two needs. The next stage is the examination of possible solutions against the background of general company objectives. One solution may be found to require the recruitment of new specialists; another may involve a heavy capital outlay; another may mean entering a market which suffers from great fluctuations in demand; and yet another may be strongly opposed by the general sales manager whose cooperation will be needed to launch the new product on the market. Drucker suggests four criteria for deciding which is the best of the possible solutions that have been analysed. These are: the risk involved related to the expected gain; the amount of effort required; the timing, especially whether a dramatic change is desirable or if a slow, one-step-at-a-time approach is more suitable; and the availability of resources, particularly of human abilities.[4]

Each solution may be found to have advantages and disadvantages. If time allows, some of these can be explored further. But even a thorough examination will usually leave imponderables, such as the effects of the new, recruited specialists on existing management, or of the amount and timing of likely market fluctuations on the product. Management will then have to decide which seems to be the best of these alternatives. Before it decides to go ahead on the selected solution, it will need to decide whether the possible advantages are worth the cost and risks involved in the uncertainties. A negative decision – not to do anything at present – may seem the wisest one. Unless top management are stern, and unusual, believers in the value of change as a management stimulus, a close balance of advantages and disadvantages may be tipped by the thought of the effort and disruption that would be involved. Many managers say they do not have time for such careful preliminary investigations. This can be a dangerous half-truth. Sometimes a quick decision is vital and often it may not be possible to find out all the available facts, but speed in itself is not always a virtue. Yet in some companies speed is the primary virtue, managers even priding themselves on 'muddling through' thus forgetting the old proverb, 'more haste less speed', which is all too often applicable in such firms.[5]

Some managers, too, may dislike the idea of analysing decisions. In the business world where so much is uncertain, flair, they hold, is more important than logic. Many decisions must rest on a judgement of the relative importance of unknown factors. But the number of such decisions is decreasing and with it the need for flair. It is decreasing because an ever increasing number of management tools, such

4. Drucker, op. cit., pp. 320–21.
5. cf. Acton Society Trust, *Management Initiative*, The Trust, London, 1961.

as market and operational research, is reducing the areas
of uncertainty in business decisions. Happily they can never
do so completely, some managers may say. True, even
though there are models for estimating the relative proba-
bilities of different degrees of uncertainty.

The analysis of decisions is one way to try and improve
their content. A quite different approach, that can be pursued at the same time, is to try and improve the quality of
the original ideas. The Americans have worried in recent years
about what they call 'creativity'. Hence their concern with
the organization man whose conformity is likely to deaden
any original idea. The new technique to encourage creativity
is 'brain-storming' which, it is hoped, will produce new ideas.
A group of people are asked to throw out any ideas which
come to them on a particular subject or problem. These
are all recorded, but not discussed at the brain-storming
session, the sole purpose of which is to produce new ideas.

RESEARCH ON DECISION-MAKING

The traditional economist's picture of the business man is of
a rational being who, under the pressure of competition,
carefully weighs the costs of one action against another and
is preoccupied with marginal costs and marginal utility.
Managers, even though they may consider this description
of business behaviour to be too academic, will probably still
stress the rational element in their decisions – although they
may allow that the decisions made by others are often not
as objective as they should be. Recently some of the economists, along with the sociologists and the psychologists,
have become interested, particularly in the USA, in studying how decisions are made in practice.

Much of this research has been on why firms decide
to invest. The reasons are shown to be so varied that probably no general theory of investment decisions could hope
to compete with the complexity of the real world.[6] The desire to maximize profits would be too simple an explanation.

6. cf. Carter, C. F., and Williams, B. R., *Investment in Innovation*,
p. 53, OUP, London, 1958.

The situation of the firm is likely to have an important influence on its decision to invest. P. W. S. Andrews and Elizabeth Brunner found, for instance, that in the United Steel Company 'Most capital expenditure is decided on general policy grounds and is more a matter of the general development of the Company and of the growth of its output than of factors relating narrowly to a particular project's earning power'.[7] Hence general considerations about the position of a company and its future growth can be more important than specific considerations of the profitability of a particular investment.

Another example of the influence of the company's situation on investment comes from a study, *Investment in Innovation* by Professors Carter and Williams. They distinguish between craft and engineering industries (divided into competitive and non-competitive) and modern industries. The managements in each, they suggest, are likely to have different attitudes to investment. For instance, firms in a competitive craft industry will 'do their best to maximize their profits, but do not usually do all the investment which is profitably open to them. Investment takes place largely because of the deterioration of existing equipment and, as costing is likely to be primitive, the incentive to invest will simply be the desire to keep going'. By contrast in ' "modern" industry, whether competitive or non-competitive, a strong pressure to invest in new types of plant or new products is created by the scientific and technical staff who, in this type of industry, have a high importance and status. The rate of technical change is usually high and, as a condition of survival, emphasis must be given to research and development and to the right choice of the investment projects suited to the firm.'[8]

In many decisions, including investment ones, a number of studies show that hopes, wishes and internal politics play an important part. The element of uncertainty in many

7. Andrews, P. W. S., and Brunner, Elizabeth, *Capital Development in Steel*, p. 356, Blackwell, Oxford, 1951.
8. op. cit., pp. 51–3.

decisions enables expectations of the results of the decision to be biased in accordance with wishes. Cost estimates, for instance, may be too optimistic. Some of these biases may be unconscious, others may be consciously manipulated by managers who want a particular decision to be taken. One study even reports the following statement: 'In the final analysis, if anybody brings up an item of cost we haven't thought of, we can balance it by making another source of savings tangible.'[9] The influence of wishes may also work retrospectively, so that the reasons given for failures may be quite different from the reality, although these reasons are widely accepted as facts. So management's wishes in decision-making may prevent an objective assessment of the value of a proposed project and, if it fails, also prevent an objective assessment – often any assessment at all – of why it failed. This points to a need for looking carefully at even generally-accepted 'facts'.

Research also suggests that the description we gave of the stages in decision-making may, like the economist's models, bear little resemblance to actual business behaviour; rather it is like the syllogism in logic, a useful tool for checking the validity of one's reasons or for discovering what has gone wrong. According to William J. Gore, reporting on some research in the USA:

... the traditional idea that a decision is an event stemming from a build-up of facts and is itself a choice between alternatives, very seldom happens. Even in what might be called forced choice situations there may be no deliberate choice. In fact it seems tenable to hold that most decisions are not aggressive choices, and that by their nature they cannot be, for the crux of a decision is not the choice between alternatives but the identification of the costly invisible consequences of such a choice and fabrication of a choice which tiptoes its way through them without setting any of them off.[10]

9. Cyert, R. M., Dill, W. R. and March, J. G., 'The Role of Expectations in Business Decision Making', *Administrative Science Quarterly*, vol. III, no. 3, p. 340, December 1958.

10. In a paper prepared for the Acton Society Trust's annual conference, 1960.

The studies described so far deal with decision-making in the company as a whole. In an interesting research,[11] Norman Martin looked at the differences between decisions at four different levels of management in a large American manufacturing company. He found that the decision situation differed in a number of ways between the levels. By 'decision situation' Martin meant the whole range from the preliminary stages, through the actual decision and implementation to verification of the correctness or incorrectness of the decision.

The main differences he discovered were in the length of the time perspective, the amount of continuity and the degree of uncertainty. Decisions at the higher levels have as one would expect a longer time perspective. From first inquiry to verification of the decision took less than two weeks in 97·7 per cent of the shift foreman's decision situations; 68 per cent of the department foreman's decision situations were completed within two weeks; 54·2 per cent of the division superintendent's; and only 3·3 per cent of the works manager's. Half of the works manager's decision situations lasted over a year; 4·3 per cent of the division superintendent's, 1.5 per cent of the department foreman's and none of the shift foreman's. This shows the striking difference in distant-time perspective between the works manager and the other three levels of management. Decisions at the higher levels tended to be discontinuous as one would expect with a long time span. There were sometimes wide gaps between the different parts of the decision situation, partly due to the manager having delegated part of the process of carrying through a decision to his subordinates. At the lower levels all the stages tend to follow each other without a time interval, or with only a short one.

The decisions at the lower levels were much more clear cut. What had to be done was more easily seen, it usually had

11. 'Differential Decisions in the Management of an Industrial Plant', *Journal of Business*, vol. 29, no. 4, pp. 249–60, October 1956. (Copyright 1956, University of Chicago.)

to be done quickly and there was less uncertainty about the result than at higher levels. At the higher levels the decision situation was much more indefinite; the time within which action should be taken was often indeterminate as it could depend upon the judgement of the total situation; what should be done was often difficult to decide because there were so many elements of uncertainty in the decision. Dr Martin's research suggests that the differences in the nature of the decisions are not evenly spaced from one management level to another. There is a much greater change between some levels. In his study the main division was between the works manager and the division superintendent. Usually the principal cleavage line between types of decisions is likely to be between the top manager(s), both of a company and of an establishment, and the managers below. This would help to explain the difficulty which many companies have in finding enough good, top managers. Many middle managers may not be able to cope satisfactorily with the much more indeterminate decisions at top-management level.

TRAINING IN DECISION-MAKING

These differences in the nature of decisions at different management levels have important implications for recruitment, training and promotion. Before a management post is filled, the types of decision which have to be taken should be known. The personality characteristics and the training that a manager will need to cope satisfactorily with indeterminate decisions is likely to be different from that required for decisions made in a short time span about concrete situations. Dr Martin suggests that in training a successor it is better to do so in an assistant position, rather than in the ordinary chain of command, provided the assistant gets experience of the actual job in the holder's absence.

The principal difficulty in training for decision-making is to give young managers experience in taking different types of decisions. One of the main arguments used in favour of considerable delegation is that it develops the ability to make decisions. Hence a flat organization, with a small number of management levels, should give more opportunity for decision-making at all levels. Some companies give their young managers experience of top-management decisions by putting them in charge of semi-autonomous units. Then the man can feel that it is his business and, its success or failure, his responsibility. Such training is popular with those senior managers who believe strongly that a man learns by doing and, above all, by his mistakes.

A few companies seek to reduce trial-and-error learning in real life by setting their managers to play business games. They give the managers experience in making decisions on all aspects of a business and simulate real life by including an element of chance. But the extent to which these games can reproduce real-life situations, and thus provide an inexpensive short cut to improving the correctness of one's decisions, is doubtful since a man's reactions are not necessarily the same when he is playing a game, as when his decisions may have personal repercussions for him and for others.

SUMMARY

Management can improve the standard of its decision-making in a number of ways:

1. By clearly defining the objectives of the business, thus setting the boundaries within which decisions will be made. If the objectives are well known it will lessen the danger of outdated management beliefs having an influence on decisions.
2. By recognizing the limitations that exist and affect its freedom of decision. These limitations stem from the social background, from economic scarcities and from people's attitudes.
3. By analysing decision-making in stages to make certain that it has: one, formulated the reasons for taking a decision and defined the problem to be solved; two, analysed the nature of the problem; and three, examined the alternative solutions and their possible consequences.

4. By being suspicious of the argument that there is no time for such an analysis.
5. By being aware of the extent to which hopes, wishes and internal politics prejudice its decisions.

People from many different academic disciplines are doing research on decision-making. From this great variety of studies we selected a few of the non-technical ones. Several of these showed that the firm's situation, including the type of industry, influenced its attitude to investment more than any assessment of the amount of return on it. Other studies showed how much decisions could be prejudiced by management wishes. Another study examined the differences in the types of decisions made at different levels of management. It concluded that they were qualitatively different. The contrast in the length of time, the discontinuity and the indeterminacy of decisions at senior levels, compared to those lower down, points to the problems of selecting and training top managers who could cope satisfactorily with these type of decisions.

6

Getting the Job Done

THE SECOND PART OF the manager's job is getting things done through people. To do so successfully, he must solve three different types of problems: those of organization, communication and cooperation. First he must allocate and coordinate the work efficiently. He must decide what to delegate, to whom, and how much. He must also decide how far he wishes to spell out responsibilities, defining in detail what he wants done. His decision will be influenced partly by the organization of the company, partly by his pattern of leadership, which we shall be discussing in the next chapter, and partly by his assessment of the capabilities and personalities of his subordinates. He will need to know whether the work is done satisfactorily, hence what forms of control he is going to use. Again he will be influenced by his own attitude to management and by his judgement of his subordinates. He may feel most comfortable with a close control so that he knows what is happening all the time, or he may prefer to encourage his subordinates to check their own performance against the standards that he lays down.

After the manager has decided what he wants done and by whom, he must convey this to his subordinates and enlist their cooperation in doing it. Unfortunately, some managers are not aware that either may cause a problem. Their attitude to implementation may be summed up as 'one gives one's subordinate an order and he carries it out'. Many difficulties come from a failure to recognize the importance of clear communication and willing cooperation. Any manager has to be concerned with both, although the forms of communication and the methods of obtaining cooperation may vary to some extent, depending upon the characteristics of both the manager and the managed. A foreman talking to an Irish navvy, for instance, will use a different language and a somewhat different approach from that of the managing director of a chemical firm talking to his scientific colleagues.

The importance of effective communication and willing cooperation is often most underrated by those managers who still attach primary importance to their technical role, whether as engineers, chemists, or accountants. Such managers may only learn slowly and painfully that people often misunderstand and may be suspicious of the manager's intentions; therefore implementation will go more smoothly and speedily if the manager takes time to explain what is wanted and to listen to any objections. The management equivalent to 'a stitch in time saves nine' is 'an explanation at the start saves confusion and delay later on'.

COMMUNICATION

Communication is successful when it is understood in the fullest sense, that is both in verbal meaning and in intention. A manager cannot become good at it by learning a number of gadgets or techniques.[1] True, he can improve his communication by clearer thinking and better presentation; knowing what one wants to say, and saying it as simply and clearly as possible will reduce the risks of misunderstanding, but they are certainly not the whole answer to how to get across what one means. There is even a danger that too much attention to communication, particularly to techniques, may distract attention from the need for cooperation, without which, good communication is useless.

Good techniques are not enough because communication, if it is to be successful in getting people both to understand and to do what is wanted, is a cooperative or two-way

1. Those who are not convinced of this should read *Is Anybody Listening?* by William H. Whyte, Jr, and editors of *Fortune*, Simon & Schuster, New York, 1952.

T—D

process. Its effectiveness depends as much, if not more, on the attitude of the recipient as on the verbal skill of the managers; on the former's ability and willingness to listen as well as on the latter's clarity and sensitivity. It also depends on whether the subordinate will say if he has not understood. Communication is, therefore, inseparably linked with co-operation. Communication is also a two-way process in a different sense in that managers not merely give advice and instructions but they also receive information on which to base their decisions. Good upwards communication is as important as good downwards communication. Both can cause difficulties for what the manager says to his subordinates may be misunderstood or misinterpreted, and what he is told may be inadequate or untrue.

Difficulties in downwards communication can arise for a number of reasons. The first need for the manager is to realize – and many do not do so sufficiently – that what he is saying is often misunderstood. He must, therefore, be prepared for such misunderstandings and, as far as possible, try to guard against them. The second is to be able to recognize their causes. Verbal misunderstandings, which are the simplest, may be due to a different use of language – especially likely when people have very different backgrounds – to lack of clarity, or to technical jargon. They may also arise from the general tendency to distort, quite involuntarily, any message passed on by word of mouth, which is illustrated in the childish game of repeating a story from person to person. A more difficult barrier to communication is caused by distrust, often leading to a wrong interpretation of what is said and to greater distortion if the message has to be passed on. Where there is an atmosphere of suspicion, even the simplest remark and the most straightforward instruction will be examined for hidden meanings. The manager may find to his astonishment that fantastic interpretations have been put on what he said or, worse, he may go on believing that his subordinates have understood him.

The frequency with which management instructions are

misinterpreted, and the nature of such misinterpretations, can be a good indication of the level of morale. Perhaps the manager should remember, even if he does not feel like acting on it, Dostoevsky's advice in *The Brothers Karamazov*: 'If the people around you are spiteful and callous and will not hear you, fall down before them and beg their forgiveness, for in truth you are to blame for their not wanting to hear you.'[2] Although, unfortunately for the manager, it may be past policies which, throwing their shadow forward, are to blame rather than anything that the present management has done.

Barriers to communication may also be created by a failure to understand that other people have different backgrounds and experience and therefore often do not see and interpret things in the same way. The more widely different the background, the greater the danger of misunderstanding. Yet even people who have similar education and social backgrounds may make different assumptions which, if not recognized, can lead to serious misinterpretations. This was illustrated in a study of four men by Tom Burns,[3] the manager of a department and the two production engineers and chief designer immediately subordinate to him, which showed that half the time the subordinates thought that their manager had given them information or advice which they could take or not as they thought best. Whereas the manager thought that he had given an instruction or a decision, which was, therefore, to be obeyed. This was a failure in communication that arose from different assumptions about the role of the manager and the amount of freedom which should be exercised by his subordinates.

Misunderstandings are most likely to arise when there are differences in values. A study by the Acton Society Trust[4] of shop floor attitudes to promotion showed, for instance, that suspicions of promotion were often due to the different

2. Quoted: Whyte, William H., op. cit., p. 21.
3. 'Directions of Activity and Communications in Departmental Executive Group', *Human Relations*, vol. VII, no. 1, 1954, p. 95.
4. *Management Succession*, op. cit., pp. 74–6.

criteria used by management and the shop floor for judging
who would make a good foreman. The shop floor gave first
importance to being a good craftsman or technician. Management emphasized leadership qualities. Such a difference
is probably irreconcilable but here, as always, it helps management to understand it and the possible suspicions which
may arise in consequence.

Managers need to be sensitive to the areas in which misunderstandings are likely. One of the most usual, and perhaps one of the most neglected, is that of promotion. Many
managers seem unaware of the amount of suspicion, speculation, and rumour that so often surrounds promotions; suspicions which are intensified when managers are very
secretive about a new appointment. Then they are surprised
if a new manager, whose appointment has caused much
speculation and resentment, does not get full cooperation.

The barriers to successful upwards communication can
be even more formidable. There is not only the risk of misunderstanding but also the danger that what the manager is
told may be incorrect or incomplete; further, he may only
be told what he has definitely asked about. In the interests
of avoiding trouble, or of not worrying him, he may receive
a simplified, edited, and sometimes wholly untrue version of
what is happening. If he does it will usually be his own fault.
He may have made his colleagues afraid to tell him the
truth, or anxious not to hurt or worry him. Or he may have
asked questions, particularly about their mates or colleagues,
which they were unlikely to answer truthfully and which,
therefore, it would have been wiser not to have asked. In the
chapter on 'People and Organization' we saw, what managers should recognize, that people tend to cover up for each
other, particularly if they are a member of the same social
group.

One barrier to upwards communication, that is often
greater than it need be, is the lack of opportunities either
formal or informal, for employees to say what they are
thinking and feeling. Management, when it wishes to explain its views and policies, has notice-boards, house jour-

nals, letters, special meetings and a public address system. Workers often have only their union which may confine itself to wage claims and grievances. Yet both management and workers may prefer to talk about a problem before it reaches the grievance stage. Joint consultation can, if properly used, provide an opportunity to do so. But too often management thinks of it as another means of explaining its policies, rather than as a useful way of finding out what its employees are thinking. Despite the limited opportunities for upwards communication between workers and management, they are usually better than the facilities which exist in private industry for junior staff and junior management to tell senior management what they are thinking. The nationalized industries have recognized the need for this and have provided consultative and negotiating machinery for all except the most senior levels of management.

Managers, because they tend to underrate the difficulties of communication, usually exaggerate the extent to which it takes place. One illustration of this is the dual assumption made by many managers, that their subordinates know what they think of them and also that they can come and discuss their careers and personal hopes and fears with them when they wish. Yet in practice the day-to-day communications between managers and their subordinates are on immediate work matters, and discussions about a subordinate's progress and career rarely, if ever, happen informally. Recognizing this some companies have introduced a formal provision for the superior to have regular discussions with each of his staff.

The appraisal and development interviews is one example of a formal provision for communication which should, if it is done properly, be a two-way one. Unless these interviews are official policy, few managers will initiate such a discussion with their subordinates since they may find it embarrassing to talk about a man's career, especially about his weaknesses. Still fewer subordinates will do so even if their manager has an open-door policy. Often the first the manager knows of one of his staff's feeling about his progress is when he comes in to say he is leaving for another job.

So far we have talked about upwards and downwards communication, but much communication also takes place horizontally. It is essential that it should do so, especially when the implementation of a decision affects several departments. Those at the same level should be able to sort out the bugs as they develop and not be prevented by isolation or jealousies from doing so. Top management should therefore try to encourage communication between departments at all levels. It can do this partly through the formal organization, by the use of inter-departmental committees. It can also try and foster informal contact by giving managers opportunities to get to know those in other parts of the business. This is one of the values of internal management training courses. We saw in the chapter on 'People and Organization' that informal organization facilitates coordination, so that if subordinates coordinate their work, the manager will have less to do.

COOPERATION

An understanding of what has to be done is necessary for successful implementation, so is a willingness to do it. Implementation may fail because the manager's subordinates or his fellow-managers do not cooperate adequately. Again, as in communication, it is helpful to be aware of the possible difficulties in enlisting cooperation. Is there likely to be opposition, if so, from whom and why? Can this opposition be overcome? Is the plan worth the time and effort that may be necessary to do so?

A wise manager knows the limits of his own authority and, as far as possible, avoids weakening his authority by trying to exercise it where it is likely to be challenged or ignored. One American firm, for instance, that was moving into a new building which had a fine, but damageable, floor, ruled that none of its female employees could wear stiletto heels at work. This rule was considered by many of the women to be an infringement of personal liberty. The opposition was such that, when last heard of, the management was worrying about how it could back down without loss of face.

Most of what we shall have to say concerns cooperation of workers, but the cooperation of other managers is also vital. Failure to obtain it may have more serious consequences than a failure with one's immediate subordinates. Subordinates who will not cooperate may resign or be sacked, but the other managers are likely to remain. Hence 'acceptability to colleagues' is now one of the prime criteria for management selection. Yet acceptability alone is sometimes too passive a quality to ensure successful implementation. Persistence, drive, and political manipulation, supported by an understanding of other managers' motives and a correct assessment of the political situation in the company, may all be necessary to get implementation of some plans.

One of the management's main worries, both now and in the past, is how to get the workers' cooperation. A common maangement pitfall in trying to do so is the desire to find a single solution. Hence the search for panaceas which for many years has been so marked a feature of management's approach to management-worker cooperation. Each new panacea is seized on enthusiastically by anxious managers. But alack for those who seek an easy solution. Experience and research show that there is no such thing. Any one of the popular answers may be of limited usefulness given reasonably good morale, but none is the whole or even a major part of the answer and probably all can make a bad atmosphere even worse. Let us look in turn at each of these attempts to promote cooperation and see what lessons can be learnt.

COOPERATION: THE PANACEAS

Joint Consultation

The advocacy of joint consultation as a way of encouraging better management-worker relations and of increasing productivity has a long history. The first official support for it in Britain came towards the end of the 1914-18 war when the Whitley committee, in a report approved by the Government, recommended that national joint councils should be voluntarily set up in any industry sufficiently organized to make that possible. These councils should, in addition to settling wages and conditions of work, discuss 'the better utilization of the practical knowledge and experience of the workpeople' and 'improvements of processes, machinery and organization, and appropriate questions relating to management and the examination of industrial experiments, with special reference to cooperation in carrying new ideas into effect and full consideration of the workpeople's point of view in relation to them'. This, like some other post-war suggestions for improving management-labour relations, was too much in advance of its time to get much support.[5] Joint consultation was practised in some companies, but the main positive result of this recommendation was the establishment of such committees in government departments, named after the original Whitley Committee, which continue to this day. (These committees are criticized within the Civil Service for their slowness in getting things done, 'waiting for Whitley'.)

The next major attempt to promote joint consultation came from the urgent need in the last war for maximum munitions production. Joint Production Consultative and Advisory Committees were set up in many munitions industries. In the words of the engineering agreement, 'The functions of the Committee' were 'to consult and advise on matters relating to productivity and increased efficiency for this purpose, in order that maximum output may be obtained from the factory'. Some of these committees continued after the war. The post-war nationalization Acts provided another boost to the establishment of joint con-

5. For example, the effective opposition of British employers to the industrial charter proposed by those who first set up the Federation of British Industries, which would have guaranteed minimum wages, granted generous redundancy payments, and provided fringe benefits.

sultative committees. These instructed the Boards to join with the unions to provide for 'the establishment and maintenance of machinery for ... the discussion of matters affecting the safety, health, and welfare of persons employed ... and of other matters of mutual interest ... including efficiency. ...' Each nationalized industry therefore established its own system of consultative committees from local to national level.

During the post-war economic crisis the government again turned to the advocacy of joint consultation as a means of improving productivity. This time the idea was much more enthusiastically received by private industry than it had been after the first World War. Lectures and pamphlets, which may be taken as an index of the amount of interest in a subject, poured forth in the immediate post-war years extolling and explaining joint consultation.

Yet, as Clegg says in his review of the history and results of joint consultation:

... Despite the advantages of statutory support in the nationalized industries, government encouragement, and the blessing of personnel management in private industry, it is much easier to write off joint consultation's subsequent history as a failure than to discover its successes.

According to their attitudes, observers expected joint consultation to increase productivity, to raise the standards of labour relations, or to improve the conditions of the workers – or perhaps all three. But it is not easy to show that joint consultation has affected any of them, and this is as true of nationalized industry as of private undertakings.[6]

The reasons Clegg gives for failure are: first, that joint consultative committees and councils are frequently bypassed; secondly, that there is no difference in principle between this kind of consultation and collective bargaining – in both, if there is disagreement, the defeated party may try to bring pressure; thirdly, and of special importance in the nationalized industries, is the limited authority of local

6. Clegg, H. A., *A New Approach to Industrial Democracy*, p. 36, Basil Blackwell, Oxford, 1960.

management, so that many queries raised by workers' representatives cannot be settled at the local level; and fourthly, that management has not made joint consultation work. Both the third and the fourth may cause feelings of frustration among the workers' representatives. In the nationalized industries a query raised at local level may have to be referred upwards to the district and even to the national level. This may take months and has even on occasion taken years before it can be decided. The unwillingness of management to make joint consultation work is likely to be specially great where managers are forced to set up committees either because of the nationalization acts or because, in private industry, of the enthusiasm of top management which may not be shared by middle management.[7]

Two things, according to Clegg, can be said with some certainty about joint consultation in private industry: it has, by and large, done best in progressive and prosperous firms; and private industry makes much less use of joint consultation than it did ten years ago. Like other panaceas, 'It is no longer considered to be the means of establishing a harmonious industrial society. Instead it is given a place as one amongst a number of "tools" of management which may be useful in dealing with some of the awkward social situations with which management may be faced.'[8] It seems clear that joint consultation works best where it is least needed – nor have the studies shown that there is a casual connexion between good labour-relations and joint consultation. Perhaps, as Clegg put it, 'A competent management can improve output and labour relations, and, if need be, also make a joint-consultative committee work.'[9]

Profit-sharing

The earliest known schemes date back to at least 1820 in France, 1860 in England and 1869 in the USA. In more recent years profit-sharing has been both more and less

7. ibid., pp. 38–41.
8. ibid., p. 38.
9. ibid., p. 37.

popular than joint consultation as a means of enlisting the workers' cooperation and promoting a sense of belonging Quantitatively less popular, a survey of the United States Bureau of Labor Statistics for 1945–6 showed that out of the 15,636 companies covered only about 300 (two per cent) had profit-sharing plans for their workers. In the UK at the end of 1954 there were, according to the Ministry of Labour Gazette,[10] 297 undertakings with profit-sharing schemes applying to all employees; this number did not include those in cooperatives. The British schemes had 321,064 participants.

Profit-sharing has been more popular in that its supporters have had even higher hopes of its value than the advocates of joint consultation. (The two are not, of course, mutually exclusive, both may be practised in the same firm.) The most important among the declared objectives of management have been, according to an International Labour Organization review of profit-sharing:[11]

1. the prevention of strikes and the improvement of the morale of the workers;
2. the provision of an effective incentive to greater efficiency and increased output;
3. the achievement of a measure of flexibility in the total payroll enabling an automatic adjustment of the total remuneration of labour to business fluctuations;
4. the reduction of labour turnover and stabilization of the labour force;
5. the promotion of thrift and a sense of security among the workers;
6. greater publicity for the firm;
7. the preservation of capitalism by giving the worker a stake in its continued existence.

In spite of this formidable list of advantages, there has been a high death rate amongst profit-sharing schemes. An

10. 'Profit-Sharing and Co-Partnership Schemes', *Ministry of Labour Gazette*, pp. 165–9. HMSO, London, May 1956.
11. Narasimhan, P. S., 'Profit-Sharing: A Review', *International Labour Review*, pp. 469–99, December 1950.

American study gave the following figures for its surveys of discontinued schemes in 1920, 1934, 1937, 1947:[12]

Proportion of Discontinued Profit-sharing Plans in the USA Plans Covered by Survey

	Active		Discontinued		Total	
Year of Survey	No. Coys	% of Total	No. of Coys	% of Total	No. of Coys	% of Total
1920	41	45.6	49	54.4	90	100.0
1934	72	47.7	79	52.3	151	100.0
1937	65	40.4	96	59.6	161	100.0
1947	167	82.7	35	17.3	202	100.0

The much lower mortality rate for 1947 is probably due partly to the great prosperity of US business during the war and immediate post-war years and partly to the desire to avoid taxation. According to the ILO review the interest in profit-sharing has tended to follow the business cycle. A 1956 American survey by the National Industrial Conference Board showed that 31·3 per cent of the plans based on current distribution had been discontinued since 1946 mainly because of union opposition.[13]

A survey of 679 plans established in the UK up to 1936 showed that 395 had been abandoned and 18 others had ceased to operate because of mergers.[14] The Ministry of Labour Survey at the end of 1954[15] had details of 605 discontinued schemes (no information was available for the years 1939 to 1953). Over one-half of these schemes lasted ten years or more. 194 were discontinued because the enterprise came to an end or was changed, for instance, through

12. 'Profit-Sharing for Workers', *Studies in Personnel Policy*, No. 97, p. 35, The National Industrial Conference Board, New York, 1948.

13. 'Sharing Profits with Employees', *Studies in Personnel Policy*, No. 162, National Industrial Conference Board, New York, 1957.

14. Balderston, C. C., *Profit-Sharing for Wage Earners*, pp. 8–9, Industrial Relations Counsellors Incs., New York, 1937.

15. *Ministry of Labour Gazette*, op. cit., p. 168.

nationalization. It is interesting that 75 were discontinued because other benefits such as increased wages or shorter hours were substituted instead.

The ILO review of profit-sharing concluded that:

The history of profit-sharing in all countries where it has been left to the voluntary enterprise, as in the United Kingdom and the United States, is full of examples of plans started with high hopes and ended in failure, sometimes after many years of operation.

In a few, rather exceptional cases it has been a spectacular success, but judging from the long list of abandoned plans and comparatively small number that have endured for more than a few years, the contribution that profit-sharing can make to the promotion of healthy and happy industrial relations and to more efficient production seems to be rather problematical.[16]

Incentive Payment Systems

The advocates of profit-sharing and joint consultation believe that these will stimulate and encourage the workers to take more interest in the company, to identify with it and therefore to wish to increase productivity. A different approach, although, again, not a mutually exclusive one, is the belief that if the worker's material advantage is linked to high productivity, he will produce more. Hence payment by results, which was for many years, and is still often today, the most popular method for enlisting workers' cooperation in high productivity.

Incentive schemes have a long history and come in many types and forms which are enthusiastically advocated and vigorously decried. The literature on the subject is immense, but much of it is too partisan to be of use in trying to find out whether and, if so, in what circumstances and in what form an incentive payment system can be of help. However, there is also a considerable amount of research results. At the suggestion of the Joint Committee on Human Relations in Industry of the Department of Scientific and Industrial Research and the Medical Research Council,

16. Narasimhan, P. S., op. cit., p. 481.

Mr Marriott of the Industrial Psychology Research Group of the MRC was asked to make a critical evaluation of previous work on the subject. The main object of the resulting book was to 'provide an outline of the present state of knowledge on incentive payment systems' excluding schemes which are not related to production, such as pension or sick pay schemes.[17]

Disappointingly for those managers who want to know in general whether incentive payments are 'a good thing', Marriott decided that it is 'possible to make certain generalizations but almost impossible to state definite conclusions regarding the overall value or efficacy of incentive payment systems'.[18] This negative conclusion is in itself of interest, for one would have little idea from reading most of the literature which advocates incentive payments that there is any doubt at all about their value. Marriott suggests that the fact that there are advocates and antagonists for each type of system and each separate scheme, as well as for or against such systems as a whole, is evidence of the lack of any clear-cut evidence in their favour. Nor is the variety of views related to their holders' vested interests.

One of the difficulties of assessing the value of incentives, according to Marriott, is that 'they have often received the credit which was due to simultaneous improvements in other directions'. The effects of these and other changes, as so many of the studies and accounts showed, were either not, or could not be, assessed. As he points out:

... A mere scanning of the lists of advantages and disadvantages claimed by experienced observers shows how elusive this problem is. Where success with a given system is claimed in one set of circumstances, failure is the result in another and the impartial judge is driven back to the conclusion that both outcomes are the results of local conditions and, probably still more, depend on the leading managerial personalities involved. Then,

17. Marriott, R., *Incentive Payment Systems: A Review of Research and Opinion*, Staples Press, London, 1957.
18. ibid. This and other quotations are taken from the final chapter 'A General Appraisal', pp. 189–206.

too, some experienced observers are convinced, and some investigations support their views, that where success is claimed it is more a matter of management having been brought face to face, not with the inefficiency of workers and the need for greater effort on their part but with the inadequacy of the organization or some aspect of it.[19]

Marriott discovered a number of trends in management's attitude to, and use of, incentive payment schemes. Specifically, there is a movement away from individual to group incentives and from both of these to longer term collective schemes. Some companies are going still further and replacing incentive schemes, in whole or in part, by controlled day work, that is, agreed flat-hourly rates of pay for well-defined work. The reasons given for these changes to controlled day work by the author of an unpublished report, an inquiry into a number of companies who had made, or were seriously considering such a change, were:

1. The realization of the need for a more human method of payment which would encourage worker responsibility and worker interest in company progress.
2. The need to replace really bad incentive schemes by payment methods which give improved relations and improved operator morale.
3. The need to replace incentive schemes which, due to extensive progress in mechanization, have largely lost their point.
4. The need to reduce administration costs.
5. The need to facilitate the introduction of sweeping changes in methods or to increase operator mobility.
6. Pressure from unions or shop representatives.
7. The need to freshen up a works atmosphere, particularly where schemes have been in operation many years.[20]

Reasons three and five stem from technical changes and are therefore no reflection on the efficacy of incentive payment schemes, but the other reasons are an indictment of such

19. ibid., p. 192.
20. White, G. H., *Incentives v. Controlled Day Work*, a private communication issued by Messrs Petfoods Ltd, Melton Mowbray, 1956. Quoted in Marriott, op. cit., p. 195.

schemes. It is possible, of course, that too much enthusiasm may be being shown for the new alternative.

Marriott also noticed a general trend over the last thirty years, and especially since the last war, to reject the panacea approach to incentive payments. Though 'the continuing widespread use of payment by results as a means of increasing productivity suggests that they are still considered to be more advantageous than otherwise'. Today, incentive schemes are much less often thought of as providing, by themselves, the necessary motivation for workers to reach an optimum level of productivity. Progressive managers now look on them, like the other panaceas, as a possible part of a much wider setting that must include human relations and technical and organizational efficiency.

This setting is all the more important since an incentive can only be effective if it increases the worker's willingness to work, as distinct from his capacity to do so, which may be increased through better equipment and organization, or through an improvement in his health. All schemes for increasing the worker's cooperation are based on the assumption – for which there is plenty of evidence – that there may be a gap, sometimes a large gap, between the worker's willingness to work and his capacity to do so. This gap is not, of course, confined to manual workers, as disincentives to effort can, and do, operate at all levels. Let us therefore turn to what is known about the worker's motivation and his willingness to work.

MOTIVATION

The incentives which management provides for its employees will depend, at least to some extent, on its views of why people work and what they want from their work. It may believe that the willingness to work is mainly influenced by external factors such as an incentive payment scheme, that people are naturally lazy and have to be motivated, pushed, and prodded to work; or it may think that the desire to work is primarily internal, that most people want to do a good day's work, but need a favourable environment in which to do it. If it thinks the former is more important it will seek for ways of devising effective incentives and means of checking that people are working hard. If it believes more in the latter it will be most concerned with trying to provide a satisfactory working environment in which people are not frustrated and can take an interest in their work. Whichever it believes, most managements now probably accept the fact that the worker's attitudes have an effect on his productivity, hence the interest in attitude surveys.

Since a large part of the manager's job is getting things done through people, it is essential for him to try to understand people's motivation. Managers tend to err in one of two directions in their expectations of how their subordinates will behave. They may expect them to react in the same way as they themselves would and think them bloody-minded if they do not; conversely they may think of their subordinates as being different human beings, with markedly different and much simpler motivations, from themselves. The latter attitude was illustrated in a study of different levels in industry – workers, foremen and general foremen.[21] Each was asked what satisfactions he most wanted from his job: the foremen and general foremen were also asked what they thought their subordinates wanted. The superiors consistently overrated the importance of economic factors to their subordinates and underestimated the importance of social satisfactions, such as 'getting along well with the people I work with' and 'a good chance to do interesting work'. The superiors would have been far more accurate in their estimates of what their subordinates wanted if they had assumed they wanted much the same as they did.

Some, indeed many, managers are certain that money is the chief incentive. They may add to this fear of the sack and deplore the fact that full employment has removed this incentive to good work. These incentives, money and fear of the sack, make the most depressing assumptions: that

21. Kahn, Robert L., 'Human Relations on the Shop Floor', in *Human Relations and Modern Management*, edited by E. M. Hugh-Jones, pp. 49–51, North-Holland Publishing Co., Amsterdam, 1958.

T—E

people are naturally lazy and have to be bribed or cowed into good work, that the only worthwhile incentives, as Professor McGregor has pointed out,[22] are those that are enjoyed off the job; therefore, people spend much of their waking life doing something they dislike so that they may enjoy the rest of the time. Happily research does not support these depressing assumptions.

Research shows that high wages are not the main incentive. There are over 150 interview studies of workers' attitudes on the job. These vary in their conclusions, as is to be expected since they cover a great variety of workers and conditions, but most of the studies show that security or steadiness of employment are the most important for the worker. Other factors which are rated higher than good wages are comfortable working conditions, a friendly and reasonable boss and pleasant social relations with fellow workers.

The conventional management view, that people are naturally lazy and, therefore, have to be bribed and prodded into activity, is being attacked by those who think that management's main task is to provide the conditions in which people's natural energies will be released. In the words of one of the foremost American writers on human relations, management's task is:

to create conditions which will generate active and willing collaboration among all members of the organization – conditions which will lead people to *want* to direct their efforts towards the objective of the enterprise ... *People often expend more energy in attempting to defeat management's objectives than they would in achieving them.* The important question is not how to get people to expend energy, but how to get them to expend it in one direction rather than another. For management, the answer lies in creating such conditions that efforts directed towards the objectives of the enterprise yield genuine satisfaction of important human needs.[23]

22. McGregor, Douglas, 'Changing Patterns in Human Relations', *Conference Board Management Record*, vol. 12, no. 9, p. 366, New York, September 1950.

23. ibid., p. 323.

NO PANACEAS, BUT A CHALLENGE TO MANAGEMENT

Our brief survey of the search for panaceas to solve all problems of management-labour cooperation shows that there are none. The belief, for instance, that payment by results is the answer to enlisting workers' cooperation in higher productivity is based on too simple a view of human motivation. Now that so many studies have shown that workers are interested in other things as well as money, that they place a higher value on social satisfactions – that is, recognition of them as people and congenial working relationships – than on take-home pay, there is a challenge to management. The challenge is to provide the conditions in which people will want to work and therefore to cooperate.

One reason why these panaceas failed to fulfil what was expected of them is that they have so often been pursued without the management philosophy that would give them a chance of contributing to better relations. Both joint consultation and profit-sharing imply a particular management-worker relationship, stemming from a philosophy of management. Without the right philosophy any scheme for improving management-worker relations is hollow; with it, any scheme can be correctly seen as a possibly useful means for expressing and implementing it, rather than as a cure-all for bad relations. This philosophy must be based on a belief in the dignity and value of each individual in the company – individuals, not hands or numbers. Such a belief will carry with it a recognition that people should be consulted before changes are made which directly affect them.

One problem that worries some top managers is how to make certain that their junior and middle managers have the same philosophy as themselves. This is particularly likely to be a problem when there is a change in top management, for instance, through nationalization or a merger. A new, more progressive, top management may find that the middle managers, especially, have quite different ideas of the way employees should be treated. Nor may top management be able to sack, or retire, even if it wishes to do so, those managers who will not, or for personality reasons cannot, cooperate, because the numbers involved may be too great. The problem will solve itself eventually as managers retire or leave, but as Keynes said, 'in the long run we are all dead'. This may be true for a company too.

Since the philosophy of management is vital to the relations which exist between management and its employees, what kind of people are made managers is one of the most important decisions to be made in a company. To this problem we shall therefore turn in the next chapter.

SUMMARY

A manager who is successful in getting decisions implemented by other people must organize efficiently, communicate clearly, and secure people's willing cooperation. One danger is that many managers underrate the difficulties of communication, of conveying to their subordinates what they want done and why, or of getting reliable information from them. Hence, they may be startled when their actions and motives are misinterpreted. Another danger is that the manager may fail to realize the need to enlist the cooperation of his subordinates. Yet another is that, although he is aware of the difficulties of doing so, he may search for some panacea such as joint consultation, profit-sharing, or incentives as *the* answer to his problems of winning cooperation.

We looked at joint consultation, profit-sharing, and incentives and saw that there is no evidence that any of them is the magic talisman which so many managers are looking for. At best, they may be a useful tool where management-worker relations are already good. So many attempts to improve worker cooperation fail because they are based on the wrong assumptions about the worker's motivation and derive from the wrong management philosophy. We saw that the problems of securing willing cooperation pose a challenge to management; a challenge to provide the conditions in which people will want to work, and, therefore, to cooperate.

7

Leadership and Development

TOP MANAGERS of progressive companies worry more – or at least more vocally – about how to ensure a supply of good managers than about any other business problem. Millions of words have been written about how to do it; fat fees are charged for attempting to educate managers, but what do we really know about it? This chapter will first take a critical look at management qualities, since listing the qualities of a good manager is the starting point for most management discussions on selection and training. Next it will look at what the research on leadership has found out which can be useful to industry. This is a source of information which is too often neglected by management. Finally, it will discuss some of the problems of management development.

MANAGEMENT QUALITIES

What are the qualities of a good manager? This is one of the most popular questions in management discussions and one which is taken very seriously. Multitudinous qualities have been said to be not merely desirable but essential for a good manager. For instance, a questionnaire-survey of 75 top executives, carried out by the American business journal, *Fortune*, listed fifteen executive qualities: judgement, initiative, integrity, foresight, energy, drive, human relations skill, decisiveness, dependability, emotional stability, fairness, ambition, dedication, objectivity, and cooperation.[1] Nearly a third of the 75 said that they thought all these

1. Stryker, Perrin, 'On the Meaning of Executive Qualities', *Fortune*, vol. LVII, no. 6, New York, June 1958.

qualities were indispensable. The replies showed that these personal qualities have no generally-accepted meaning. For instance, the definitions of dependability included 147 different concepts. Some executives even gave as many as eight or nine. Nor are British top managers any less demanding in the qualities which they require for a good manager, or better agreed as to their meaning.

The usual lists of vague, undefined qualities are no help in management selection and development. They also call for paragons, whereas all companies must make do with imperfect human beings. However, there have been attempts to make more carefully defined lists based on observation. Two of the more thought-provoking of these lists are given below. The first is of the characteristics of successful business men compiled by Professors Edwards and Townsend, who say that 'in varying combinations and proportions these qualities seem to be found in the leadership of most businesses that have grown substantially.'[2]

1. Strength and willingness to work hard, immensely hard in some cases;
2. Perseverance and determination amounting at times to fanatical single-mindedness;
3. A taste and flair for commerce, an understanding of the market-place;
4. Audacity – a willingness to take risks that are sometimes large gambles;
5. Ability to inspire enthusiasm in those whose cooperation and assistance is essential;
6. Toughness amounting in some men to ruthlessness.

Lewis and Stewart looking at the literature on successful business men found that two qualities stood out: optimism and self-confidence. Yet these qualities alone are obviously not sufficient to make for success in business.[3] The second

2. Edwards, Ronald S., and Townsend, Harry, *Business Enterprise: its growth and organisation*, p. 33, Macmillan, London, 1958.

3. Lewis, Roy, and Stewart, Rosemary, *The Boss: The Life and Times of the British Business Man*, p. 104. Phoenix House, London, revised edition, 1961.

list is compiled by Professor Argyris.[4] It is limited to characteristics which he thinks are helpful in becoming and remaining a successful executive operating in competitive conditions. The characteristics are drawn from observing numerous American executives, so would not all be possessed by any one executive. This is in contrast to the previous list which was of qualities likely to be found in most successful business men. Argyris's list is:

1. Exhibit a high tolerance of frustration;
2. Encourage full participation and are able to permit people to discuss and pull apart their decisions without feeling that their personal worth is threatened;
3. Continually question themselves, but without being constantly critical of themselves;

    These executives, we would like to emphasize, were keenly aware that their personal biases, their personal ways of seeing the world, were not necessarily the only or the best ways ... They respected their own judgement, not as always being correct, but as always being made with the best possible intentions. Their self-respect seemed to enable them to respect others.

4. Understand the 'laws of competitive warfare' and do not feel threatened by them;
5. Express hostility tactfully;
6. Accept victory with controlled emotions;
7. Are never shattered by defeat;
8. Understand the necessity for limits and for 'unfavourable decisions';
9. Identify themselves with groups, thereby gaining a sense of security and stability;
10. Set goals realistically.

These two lists portray widely different personalities. In part this is because the first list was compiled by economists and the second by a man who is a psychologist and sociologist. It is noteworthy what very different qualities they select as being important. So much so, that it is likely that even if they had been looking at the same people they would

4. Argyris, Chris, *The Personnel Journal*, vol. 32, no. 2, pp. 50–55, June 1953.

still have emphasized different qualities as the reasons for success. The contrasts between these two approaches have wider implications. They show the key role played by the company recruiters of potential managers; the character of future managers will be affected by the qualities they looked for, which will vary with the individual recruiter.

The contrasts between the two lists is also due to a difference in the kind of successful executive who is being analysed. The first list seems to be limited to the heads of companies; the second list seems to include managers at different levels. (Neither of the authors are very specific on this point.) The former deals with the entrepreneur, the latter with the company man – the professional manager. Both lists could be useful, in different circumstances, in the examination of promotion potential. But it would be essential to know what kind of top manager was needed. This would depend upon the situation of the company and on the stage in its development. These we shall discuss later.

RESEARCH ON LEADERSHIP

One of the most important findings of the research is that there is not *one* leader's job. This puts the question, 'What are the qualities of the good manager?' in a new perspective since research shows that different situations require different leadership qualities and therefore different types of leaders. Hence, there is no one type of good manager, nor one set of qualities which a good manager will possess. This will be borne out by anyone with a wide experience of industry who has noticed the great diversity of character among successful managers. This finding should prompt the man who is trying to fill a management vacancy to ask, 'What is the nature of this particular job?' 'What are its distinctive problems?' and, therefore, 'What kind of manager is needed to fill it?' Unfortunately the answer to these questions cannot be precise because so little is known about which characteristics of a job are important.

Although our knowledge of what important differences

affect the nature of the manager's job is limited, we can point to some differences which are likely to be important. These come both from the nature of the organization itself, both formal and informal, and from the external demands made on the organization. The manager in a highly structured organization will have a different type of authority from the man in a very informal one. The man who is happy managing in a bureaucracy might be very uncomfortable in a more informal and democratic set-up. The job of managing a stable, well-established company with an assured market, in so far as there is such a thing, is different from that of running – the change in verb is itself indicative of the difference – a new company in a highly competitive market. This difference was discussed by H. P. Barker, chairman and managing director of Parkinson and Cowan Ltd, who made an interesting distinction between arrival and survival leaders:

It seems to me that the kind of organization required for 'arrival' is different from that which is subsequently required to ensure the survival of the already arrived. It is certainly true that small businesses have the highest 'arrival potential' value as measured by the rates of growth of which they are capable. It is equally true that large businesses have a higher survival value than small.

A management which aims to arrive must have as its main asset a leader with an *idée fixe* and a ruthless determination to succeed. A management which aims to survive must possess an executive which will prevent first degree mistakes and which will create the kind of climate in which the right things tend to happen at operational executive levels.

If this generality is accepted then clearly a group of companies should be organized so that each operating subsidiary has a management designed for the 'arrival' of their own unit, whereas the group executive should be designed to ensure the survival of the group as a whole.[5]

The qualities described by Edwards and Townsend are those of an 'arrival' manager.

5. Barker, H. P., in a London School of Economics Seminar paper, May 18, 1948, quoted by Edwards and Townsend, op. cit., pp. 200–201

There are a number of examples of boards of directors which decided that their company had reached the survival stage and sacked or prematurely retired the managing director who had been responsible for the company's arrival, because they thought that he would not be a good leader for this next stage. This is somewhat similar to the different qualities required for a nation's leader in times of war compared with a peace-time leader.

Although the nature of the leader's job varies, are there some things that all good leaders do? This is one of the questions which has interested research workers on leadership. The Ohio State University, the centre for one of the major groups which has studied leadership, in 1946 started a ten-year interdisciplinary programme to study the behaviour of leaders in business, education, and government. They decided that trying to define the qualities of a good leader was unsatisfactory, and sought instead to define leadership in terms of performance. After a lot of work they finally reduced the basic functions of a good leader to two:

1. *Consideration of human relations,* that is, 'the extent to which the executive, while carrying out his leadership functions, is considerate of the staff'.
2. *Initiating structure or 'get the work out',* that is 'the executive organizes and defines the relationship between himself and the members of his staff. He tends to define the role which he expects each member of the staff to assume and endeavours to establish well-defined patterns of organization, channels of communication, and ways of getting jobs done'.[6]

The original research concerned bomber pilots,[7] but the same dimensions seem to exist in industry and in educational administration. A good leader should be above average in developing warm relations with his staff and in

6. Shartle, Carroll L., *Executive Performance and Leadership,* op. cit., pp. 120–22.
7. Halpin, Andrew W., 'The Leadership Behaviour and Combat Performance of Airplane Commanders', *Journal of Abnormal and Social Psychology,* vol. XLIX, no. 1, pp. 19–22, January 1954.

initiating new ways to solve problems. But the relative importance of the two will vary in different types of work.

There is a conflict between human relations and getting the work out; a conflict known to many managers. Subordinates demand that their manager should be both powerful and popular, that he should both initiate ideas and move his group towards the goal on the one hand, and be considerate on the other.[8] The conflict may be resolved by sharing the roles between two leaders, so that one leader is powerful – he gets things done – and the other is popular and looks after the social and emotional needs of the members. One often sees this sharing of leadership qualities, particularly at the top of an organization. It is helpful for the manager to be aware of the existence of this conflict and therefore of the nature of the choice before him. It may also help him in the selection of his deputy, particularly if he is weak on one of the two; he should probably choose a deputy who can complement him. If the manager is unaware of this conflict he may fluctuate in his attempts to satisfy first one demand and then the other. Whereas, what he has to make certain is that both demands are being satisfied within the group, not that he necessarily satisfies them himself.

There are also conflicts between what superiors and subordinates want of the manager. It is difficult for a manager to fulfil the expectations of both and be liked by both. Subordinates are likely to want supervisors who are considerate, while superiors want managers to be primarily concerned with achieving the goals of the organization. This conflict is greatest at the foreman level, since the foreman may be the buffer between the conflicting aims of management and workers.

The discussion about complementary leaders, resolving the conflict between being powerful and popular, points to another of the findings of the research on leadership: the leadership qualities that are needed in any particular situation are not concentrated in one individual, but are spread among several. Nor is leadership, in terms of the ability to

8. Shartle, op. cit., p. 125.

influence others, necessarily identical with formal status. We all know that the amount of influence that a person exerts is a combination of his position and his personality. We saw, for instance, in the chapter on 'People and Organization', how certain weaknesses of the managing director in one company were complemented by the strengths of one of the managers reporting to him.

Those responsible for selecting a new manager need to consider not merely his strengths and weaknesses but also those of his future colleagues. This raises most problems when a new managing director is being appointed. Does top management need a thorough shake-up? Unless it does, will the existing people be able to adjust to the new man's leadership pattern? If not, will their resignations or difficulties hurt the company? The tendency of newly-appointed leaders to replace some of their subordinates may be explained by the need to find people who complement them. A manager should also know his own weaknesses and seek to make up for them in the selection of his staff. In this sense there may be some truth in the dictum that 'a good manager can manage anything', because he will try to build up a team that balances his own deficiencies in knowledge and personality.

One of the questions asked by the research workers on leadership, that is obviously relevant to management training, is, 'What are the effects of different methods of leadership?' Much of the research has tried to compare the effects of a democratic leader – that is, one who encourages participation – with those of an authoritarian leader. Most of it points towards the desirability of the democratic type of leader who encourages participation, places employee welfare before production, but does not give the former undue emphasis, and exercises only a general rather than a close supervision.[9] Later research also showed that a supervisor

9. cf. a summary of the major research in this subject, carried out by the Institute of Social Research, University of Michigan, given by Rensis Likert in *New Patterns of Management*, pp. 5–43, McGraw-Hill, New York, 1961.

can be too employee-centred and that this may lead to low production and low morale.

Recently, doubts have been expressed about the feasibility of democratic leadership in industry. Partly because of the hierarchical structure of industry, and partly because it is harder to be democratic in an organization where some of the power lies outside, as is true in business, where the customers and the government can, and do, exert pressure. An alternative to democratic or authoritarian leadership has been suggested by Professor Argyris which he calls 'reality-centred' stressing that:

Effective leadership depends upon a multitude of conditions. There is no one predetermined, correct way to behave as a leader. The choice of leadership pattern should be based upon an accurate diagnosis of the reality of the situation in which the leader is embedded.[10]

The manager who is trying to decide what is the best way for him to manage might turn to 'How to Choose a Leadership Pattern' by Robert Tannenbaum and Warren H. Schmidt.[11] They suggest that there are three factors which the manager should take into account: his own characteristics; those of his subordinates; and those of the situation.

The manager's characteristics which are important in deciding how to manage are:

1. His value system, including his views on whether individuals should have a say in decisions affecting them; the importance he attaches to efficiency; the personal growth of his subordinates and company profits.
2. His confidence in his subordinates.
3. His own leadership inclinations, whether he is more comfortable being a member of a team or being highly directive.
4. His feelings of security in an uncertain situation, hence his ability to delegate without feeling too worried about the resulting uncertainty of the outcome. 'This "tolerance for

10. 'Personality and Organization', op. cit., p. 207.
11. *Harvard Business Review*, vol. 36, no. 2, pp. 95–101, March–April 1958.

ambiguity" is being viewed increasingly by psychologists as a key variable in a person's manner of dealing with problems.'

The characteristics of the subordinates which are important are:

1. The strength of their need for independence.
2. Their readiness to assume responsibility for decision-making.
3. Their tolerance for ambiguity; some subordinates have a preference for clear-cut directives, others prefer more freedom.
4. Their interest in the problem and their views on its importance.
5. Their degree of understanding of, and identification with, the goals of the organization.
6. Their knowledge and experience.
7. Whether they have learned to expect a share in decision-making.

The amount of freedom that the manager can allow his subordinates will depend upon the extent to which there is a positive answer to the above points.

The characteristics in the situation that are important are:

1. The type of organization, including: the kind of behaviour which is customary, and the limitations placed on employee participation by the size of the establishment, the geographical distribution and the degree of organizational security which is necessary.
2. Group effectiveness; this is important when the delegation is to the group, rather than to an individual.
3. The nature of the problem; for instance, if the manager has most of the information which is relevant, it may be easier for him to think it through himself rather than to brief one or more of his staff.
4. The amount of time available to make a decision will affect the extent to which the manager feels that he can involve his subordinates in decision-making.

The authors conclude that the successful leader is one who is both keenly aware of the factors which are relevant to his behaviour at a particular time, and who is also able to act appropriately. He is both perceptive and flexible. This means that when the situation calls for it, he will be a strong leader, in different circumstances he will be a permissive one.

DEVELOPING MANAGERS[12]

Some, although a decreasing number of, managers believe that good managers are born and that little or nothing needs to, or can, be done to help their development, since this will be a natural process of a potentially good manager learning by experience and example. 'You cannot keep a good man down' is their motto, allied to the belief that he will learn for himself whatever the circumstances. Managers who believe this are obviously not concerned with the problems of how to develop their subordinates. But the number who hold this comforting belief is steadily decreasing. The others are often worried men: conscious of the increased demands made on management by the growing size and complexity of industry, as well as by the change in the type of people who are managers, they look anxiously round for the men who have the potential to meet these demands. Once found, how are they to be given the necessary training and experience? A still more worrying question is, what *is* necessary?

There would probably be considerable support for a general statement such as: 'A manager should first have a knowledge of a specific function, including both theoretical training and experience on the job. Next he must understand management tools, such as budgetary control and standard costs.' A professional background and a grasp of the tools of management are the easy part of the answer to the question, 'What training and experience is necessary for a good manager?' Difficulties arise when we think of the core of the manager's job – managing people and making decisions – and consider whether education and training can help to improve his performance on both.

A distinction is frequently made between training to improve a man's performance in his present job and education

12. This is a brief discussion. The author has written in more detail in Acton Society Trust's *Management Succession*, op. cit.

for promotion. A distinction abhorred by Peter Drucker who argues that all training should be for development to meet tomorrow's demands, and that the concept of an elite with high potential is a fallacy.[13] We cannot, he argues, predict a man's development more than a short time ahead, and we have no right to dispose of people's careers on probability. This is an admirable warning, but large firms may have to judge that one man is more likely to reach the top than another if they are to give their future managers sufficient experience on the way up. Some distinctions on promotability are probably necessary, but they can be made without creating a permanent elite.

Those who do distinguish between training to improve performance and education for promotion, think of the former as being concerned with technical knowledge and the tools of management, including the ability to write and speak clearly and effectively. It may also include an attempt to change attitudes to management. Education for promotion is described as broadening – the subject of an immense amount of discussion.

Broadening, whether thought of solely in relation to promotion, or as something that should be the aim of all management education, means a deepening of understanding rather than an increase in the amount of knowledge. Such an understanding should cover three areas. First, the manager must understand the nature of the external environment and its effects on the company which can range from government regulations, and the character of the trade unions in the industry, to the general economic situation and the market conditions affecting the firm. In a company with overseas interests, the manager may also need to understand something of the economic and social facts in the relevant countries as well as their differences in outlook. Secondly, he must learn to see the business as a whole and the role and problems of each department. Thirdly, his understanding of people's reaction must be deepened, as well as being extended, to include different types of people

13. op. cit., pp. 159–61.

from those he may have dealt with on the shop floor or in the offices. He will have to learn how to manage managers. Both those who work for him and, using the word 'manage' in a different sense, his peers who may be competing with him for promotion, for status, and for scarce resources. Broadening should make a manager more aware of all the factors which influence his job and his company, more aware of his own reactions and more perceptive of other people's, and more flexible in his approach. But it is one thing to describe in very general terms what is meant by broadening, another to know how to achieve it, or to know whether there is any general prescription or only individual ones.

One method which is used, although not nearly so frequently as it is advocated, is job rotation. Those who favour it argue that it widens a man's experience and should make him more flexible. Some also believe that, if a man is to get the necessary experience for top management, his experience must be planned and accelerated, and that, if he is to get quickly enough up the management ladder, he must be singled out for such planned experience. Some companies try to ensure that a man gets a variety of different types of jobs by moving him from one department to another, by sending him to visit other companies, especially abroad, or by putting him in a job which gives him a general view of many aspects of the business. The use of this form of development is restricted by the price, which may have to be paid in temporary dislocation, when a person with no knowledge of a department is put into a vacant post in preference to a suitable person already in that department. The companies which use job rotation as a conscious policy are likely to have a general policy of moving people in their early years and later to practise selective job rotation. One of the very large British companies occasionally creates vacancies in order to develop those earmarked for top management. For others with potential it tries to use suitable vacancies when they arise. Job rotation as a means of developing a manager by widening his experience is fairly straightforward, although there is much we do not know about the mechanics: how long should be spent in the different jobs and what kind of transfers between departments are desirable and practicable?

The area of uncertainty becomes much greater – although some people think they know the answer without offering any evidence of its validity – when we turn to management development by formal education. Management education, in the form of courses, is increasingly considered to be a good thing, hence the done thing, if one is demonstrably running a progressive firm. Yet we know little about what kind of education is required and still less about how it can most effectively be provided. There are two main queries. What does a manager need to know? What should be his attitude to managing, and if he does not have the right attitudes, how can education help to change them? These questions concern the aims of management education. They are fundamental. But there are also important queries about methods. On the first question, what a manager should know, there is plenty of scope for disagreement on detail, but there is some agreement on the broad outline which we discussed earlier in this chapter. The research on leadership can help us to answer the first part of the second question. That is, 'What should be the manager's approach to managing?' But the main problem of management development lies in the second part: can we change attitudes, and if so, how? Many companies, for instance, are worried about how to develop an understanding of, and sensitivity to, people; how to change a good scientist or technician, who has been primarily concerned with things, into a manager who is sufficiently interested in and aware of people to be sensitive to their reactions, and to be able to adjust his behaviour accordingly.

There is little evidence about the effects of management education on attitudes. Much of the research on effectiveness of management education is inconclusive, partly because of the great difficulty of finding ways of assessing it. However, several studies of the effects of human relations

courses for supervisors show that the behaviour of the foreman's boss was very important. If his boss was considerate
this had much more effect on the foreman's behaviour than
training courses in human relations.[14]

We do know that attitudes can be changed by drastic
means, such as the brain-washing of Western prisoners in
China, or the methods used to change the attitudes of a man
or woman entering a monastery or a convent. In a most
interesting article, 'Management Development as a Process
of Influence', Professor Schein uses these extreme examples
to illustrate the process of changing attitudes.[15] This process
he says has three phases. First, unfreezing of present attitudes so that the individual is ready to change. This can be
accomplished either by increasing the pressure to change or
by reducing some of the threats or resistance to change.
Secondly, the actual change of attitude; the person learns
new attitudes either by identifying with and emulating some
person holding these attitudes, or by being placed in a situation where new attitudes are demanded of him as a way of
solving problems which he cannot avoid. Thirdly, refreez-
ing, that is the new attitudes become part of the personality.

Professor Schein thinks that unfreezing, or willingness to
change one's attitudes, is not likely to be achieved in
appraisal interviews or by management training conducted
at the place of work, because both these are too related to
the manager's normal routine. He thinks that management
courses in residential centres, where the man is isolated from
the pressures of daily life, are more likely to provide the
setting in which a man may become willing, and able, to
change. Much will depend on the atmosphere of the course,
and the support it gives to efforts at self-examination. But
the possibility of any change lasting will depend upon the
situation to which the manager returns. If he goes to a
different job, or if several of his fellow-managers go on a

14. cf. Fleishman, R. A., 'Leadership Climate and Supervisory
Behaviour', Personnel Research Board, Ohio State University, 1951.
15. Schein, Edgar H., *Industrial Management Review*, vol. II, no. 11,
May 1961.

similar course, there is more chance of it doing so. Job rotation can help to unfreeze attitudes and thus make a change of attitudes easier. A move from one setting to another removes many of the supports of the old attitude, thus giving the manager an opportunity to try new ways of behaving and to be exposed to different attitudes.

Professor Schein suggests that a course just before a man goes to a new job might provide the greatest opportunity for learning and modifying his attitudes and behaviour. A post as personal assistant, where a good relationship develops, will influence the younger man to adopt the attitudes of the older, but he will not learn new methods of looking at management problems. Hence, if a broad view is required, job rotation can expose the young manager to a variety of points of view. But working as an assistant to the right man can help a young manager to develop a quality which many British managers seem to lack; that of moral courage in dealing with their subordinates.

The uncertainties about the aims and methods of management education are, or should be, increased by the fact that management consists of so many different jobs and that it is demonstrably possible to manage successfully in many different ways. The very diversity of successful managers must make one pause before offering a general prescription for either what is a successful manager, or how he should be developed. But the research on leadership indicates that one can say, in very general terms, that a good manager is perceptive and flexible and that therefore his experience and formal education should be planned to try and develop these qualities.

HOW IMPORTANT IS A GOOD MANAGER?

We have talked so far as if producing good managers is of key importance to the success of a company. In doing so we have mirrored the views of many top managers today. Yet there is a danger that the current enthusiasm for management selection and development may place too much emphasis on the man and too little on the organization. We may be trying to find a cure for the failings of management through management education, when our attention ought first to be directed to the organization in which the manager has to work. How a manager manages is only partly due to the kind of person he is, for his behaviour is also affected by the position in which he is placed. We saw in the chapter on 'Getting the Job Done' that many of the failings which are attributed to the personality of the individual are really caused by the position in which he is placed and the pressures imposed upon him.

Some of the research on leadership has also tried to find out how jobs and organizations influence the leader's behaviour. So far there has not been enough research to be certain of the answer, but one of the smaller studies of the Ohio State research group attempted to predict how naval officers would behave in new jobs on the basis of: (1) their previous job performance and (2) the performance of their predecessor in the new job.[16] Their general finding was that the way a man would behave in a new job could be forecast almost as well by looking at the behaviour of the present job holder, as by looking at the new leader's past performance. This, if it is confirmed by other studies, is very important for our knowledge of what influences management behaviour. The conclusion Shartle, who was one of the authors, drew was that 'less than half' of leadership performance 'could be ascribed to the man and a little over half to the demands of the particular job'.[17]

Although we must continue to do all we can to improve the selection and training of managers, this research suggests that we should not think of good managers as the sole, or even necessarily the most important, factor in successful management. According to the authors of a book which summarizes much of the research that has been done:

16. Stogdill, Ralph M., *et al.*, 'A Predictive Study of Administrative Work Patterns', *Research Monograph*, no. 85, Bureau of Business Research, The Ohio State University, 1956.

17. Shartle, op. cit., p. 94.

The belief that a high level of group effectiveness can be achieved simply by the provision of 'good' leaders, though still prevalent among many people concerned with the management of groups, now appears naïve in the light of research findings.[18]

SUMMARY

There is no one management job, hence no one best type of manager. The preoccupation with vague lists of management qualities is meaningless, unless they are made more precise and related to the kind of management job that has to be done.

The findings of the research on leadership are relevant to management selection and training. These show that the basic functions of a good leader are only two: consideration and initiating structure, that is getting the work out. A good leader should be above average on both, although their relative importance will vary with the kind of job to be done. These two tend to create competing demands for the leader to be powerful and popular, but this conflict can be resolved by sharing the leadership role. Related to this, the research showed that the leadership qualities needed in any particular situation are not concentrated in one individual, but spread among several. Therefore, the strengths and weaknesses of the person who is being appointed should be considered along with those of the people he will be working closely with. Finally, the job of the manager, like that of any leader, is conditioned by the situation in which he has to manage. A good manager must be both perceptive of the situation and flexible in his ability to adapt his methods of managing accordingly.

Management education can be divided into the acquisition of specific information and the deepening of understanding. The latter, commonly called broadening, covers three areas: one, an awareness of the external environment of the firm and its effects on the company; two, an

18. Cartwright, Dorwin, and Zander, Alvin, *Group Dynamics: Research and Theory*, p. 487, Tavistock Publications, London (second edition) 1960. Row, Peterson, Evanston, Illinois, 1953.

understanding of the company as a whole and of the inter-relationships of departments and three, a greater insight into people's reactions at all levels.

So far we know little about how to broaden a manager. Job rotation is well accepted as one means of widening a man's experience and understanding, but it is not widely used in practice in most British companies. Formal management courses are still largely a gesture of faith as it is extremely difficult to assess the value of a course. So far there is little evidence that attitudes can be changed by formal courses in human relations. We do know that the environment to which the man returns is likely to have a much greater effect than the course. There is a danger that we may look to management education as a cure for problems which have their causes in bad organization.

PART THREE

Contrasts in Management

In Part Three we shall look at some of the contrasts in the manager's job. We shall see how greatly it varies according to the situations of the company and the prevailing codes of behaviour. The first chapter describes how both the time and the place affect the ways in which a manager thinks and acts. A Japanese or a French manager will often take different decisions from a British manager in the same position. The British manager today will manage differently from his predecessor a hundred years ago. The second chapter discusses some of the problems inherent in managing a large organization. In the last chapter we look at the way in which rapid change can revolutionize the nature of the manager's job.

8

Management and Social Climate

MANY MANAGEMENT textbooks are written in abstract terms about what managers do and how they do it, but few are concerned with the real-life situations of what managers actually do, still less with why they do it. Once one begins to look at the 'why' of managers' actions one finds that many of them are influenced by their particular environment. This is true both of the way in which managers behave to other people and of the type of business decisions which they take. How they treat their workers, their junior staff, each other, their directors and their customers, will partly depend on their character, but still more on what is customary at the time in their industry, locality, and country. Whether they seek to expand their businesses rapidly, to undercut their competitors, to misrepresent their products, or to put customer satisfaction before economic production will again, at least partly, depend on the prevailing mores.

THE APPROACH TO BUSINESS

What managers strive for, and the rules they observe in doing so, will be influenced, and often determined, by the accepted goals and mores in their society. All managements must be interested in profits, if they are to survive in normal circumstances. But what importance they attach to them and how they seek to achieve them will vary in different societies and at different stages in the same society. Economic goals, such as maximum profits, an expanding share of the market, greater productivity and lower costs, will be modified by social goals, such as offering an assured livelihood to long-term employees, even if this means retaining the inefficient, or not causing economic hardship by forcing one's competitor out of business.

In a rapidly industrializing society, managers, whether in private or public industry, are the path-makers, who will change or destroy many of the old ways of life. Yet the extent to which business determines the goals of a society varies greatly from one industrial country to another. Perhaps only in America could the head of a nation say, 'The Business of America is Business.'[1] In terms of a country's livelihood this is truer of the U K, but business is still not the core of British society, nor are business men the major influence in setting the society's goals. One test of whether business mores dominate society might be whether the explanation of an action as 'good business' is considered sufficient justification of its ethics. Such an explanation would be more acceptable in the USA than in the UK and more acceptable in the UK than in France. Many common business practices in the UK would be called dishonest by the man in the street. Most of these aim to mislead the consumer into thinking, for instance, that a pack is larger or a guarantee more valuable than it is.

Recently observers have commented on the differences between American, British, French, Russian and Japanese managers, to mention only a few. After the last war, British teams of managers, trade unionists and technicians visited the same industries in the USA, under the auspices of the Anglo-American Productivity Council. They enthused about the atmosphere of American business: the greater optimism, cost consciousness and continual search for improved methods.[2] Americans at all levels are, they reported, more productivity-minded. Previous foreign observers had said the same thing. To the critical, whether American or foreign, this is due to a worship of material progress, to a

1. President Coolidge, in a message to the Nation, 1924.
2. For a general description of the reports of these teams see Hutton, Graham, *We Too Can Prosper: The Promise of Productivity*, Allen & Unwin, London, 1953.

belief that the size of the gross national product is the best guide to a country's progress.

The British productivity teams, impressed by, rather than critical of, the greater American concern for productivity, sought for explanations of this difference in attitude. They found them in the greater mobility, both social and geographical, of American society; the higher status of the business man and the greater support given to the making of profits and the accumulation of capital; the greater competitiveness, both between companies and individuals and the more practical, technical orientation of American education. They also pointed to the widespread desire for a higher standard of living and the part played in this by the American woman:

In this competition for a higher standard of life it is undoubtedly the American woman who is the pacemaker.

In the striving for higher wages, based on higher productivity, the American worker has unquestionably well 'prepared himself unto the battle', and the trumpet sounded by his wife, and to which his unflagging efforts are often the valiant response, does not give 'an uncertain sound' ... viewed from the standpoint of high national industrial productivity, the influence, in this way, of the American woman must be regarded as distinctly valuable.[3]

The status of the American manager is much higher than that of his European counterpart. This has important repercussions, both on recruitment and on the attitudes of top managers. In societies where social prestige is determined by social origins and occupation, rather than by one's standard of living, the drawing-power of industry's high salaries will be less. British business as a career has suffered, until recently, from the greater prestige of the Civil Service and the professions, but now business, or at least big business, is becoming more respectable. If successful business men have a high status in their society they will probably be content to devote their energies to business. But in a society like the British, where greater prestige still attaches to other

3. Anglo-American Productivity Council, 'Internal Combustion Engines', *Productivity Team Report*, p. 7, 1949.

occupations, the ambitious and successful business man who wants a title is likely to devote an increasing amount of his time to public activities.

Competition, both between companies and individuals, varies considerably from one country to another. In part this is a result of external pressures. In the U S A companies are often forced, by anti-trust laws, to be more competitive than they would choose. In part the amount of competition depends upon business mores and the ruthlessness with which a company will seek to expand its share of the market. In a country such as France, a business man can say:

Do you mean to tell me that you can respect a man who has become wealthy through the ruin of half a dozen competitors? Such a man is a menace to society.[4]

Others may be restrained from doing so, if only for fear of the judgement of their peers. Also, as we shall see later, many French business men are less interested in expansion than their English-speaking brothers. The amount of competition between individuals, and the degree to which inefficiency is tolerated, is also strongly influenced by the kind of society in which industry grows up. Competition between individuals is stronger in the U S A than in Britain and much stronger in either than in Japan. In the U S A the inefficient manager will be fired more readily than in Britain. In the latter, the incompetent but long-service manager may be kicked upstairs and given a job with a high-sounding title, but which does not let him handicap the firm's efficiency. His livelihood and his feelings will have been spared. In Japan, where the preservation of individual status and prestige is much more important than with us, this practice is the customary one.[5] Promotion is largely by seniority at all levels. The incompetent executive is also spared any loss of face by the acceptance of group responsibility for all decisions.

4. Sawyer, J. E., 'Strains in the Social Structure of Modern France', *Modern France* (ed. Earle, E. M.), p. 324, Princeton University Press, 1951.

5. Abegglen, James C., *The Japanese Factory: Aspects of its Social Organization*, The Free Press, Glencoe, Ill., 1958.

The attitude to expansion also depends upon what business men consider important, and their concept of importance will be conditioned by the society in which they live. The attitude of the French owner-manager to expansion is markedly different from that of the American or even the British. Above all he wishes to retain family control. Hence, expansion can only come out of profits, since even bank credit may be looked on with suspicion. The Frenchman will also attach less importance to expanding his business, because far less than the American or even the British does he regard business as a way of life.

THE BACKGROUND OF MANAGEMENT

What managers think, and how they behave, are partly determined by their environment, the country, the stage of industrialization, the locality, and the industry. They are also influenced by the managers' background which is, in itself, a product of their environment. The social and educational background of managers, and the experience they obtain, will depend upon a variety of social and historical facts, such as how industry started in their country, the stage of industrialization, the status of industry in society, the importance attached to different occupations and the nature and strength of the barriers to occupational mobility. The background of the early owners and managers have differed from one country to another.

Where the family has played an important part in the growth of business and still holds many of the top jobs this may make, as in France, for conservatism. But family management is not necessarily conservative as the history of some of the British and German industrial families has shown. A study of German business showed that where the father has a wide technical or professional education, allied to a belief in hard work and determination to acquire or maintain power, he may press his sons and sons-in-law to equip themselves properly for their future responsibilities.[6]

6. cf. Hartmann, Heinz, *Authority and Organization in German Management*, ch. 6, Princeton University Press, 1959.

Then the family business will push industrialization.

In many countries, family connexions are important for getting into management posts. In some, such as India, top management posts may be restricted to a few families.[7] Hence, the power of the family in business can largely prevent management or, at least, top management from being a career open to the talents. In most countries, family management is being increasingly replaced by professional management, though the extent to which this is true varies for historical and taxation reasons. Family control has so far proved much more lasting in Germany and Japan than in Britain or the USA.

The professional background of top managers is likely to affect their judgement of what is important, hence, company policy. If, as in Germany, engineers predominate they will probably emphasize production and pay little attention to marketing. Where, as in many large British companies, accountants play an important part in top management they may be chiefly concerned with the financial standing of the firm since this affects the ease with which the company can raise capital. The proportion of university graduates among the managers may also affect the attitude to management. Unfortunately reliable comparative figures are not available, but we do know that the proportion is smaller in the UK than in the USA, even when allowances are made for differences in the standard of some graduates. We also know that the level of education of German managers is very high, compared with other countries.

Where graduates are recruited, the jobs they will actually be able to do will be restricted by the strength of local traditions and the extent to which graduates and workers share a common background. It is much more common for graduates to work as foremen in American than in British industry. This is partly due to the larger number of college graduates in the USA, and partly to the greater possibility of graduates and workers being able to talk the same lan-

7. Mehta, M. M., *Structure of Indian Industries*, pp. 260–62, Bombay Popular Book Dept., 1955.

guage. The American graduate is more likely to have gone to the same, or a similar, school and to have spent his university vacations working as an operative. In Japan, according to Abeglen, the gulf of understanding can be too wide to bridge:

The role of tradition, superstition, and local custom in the actual mining operations is very great, and the men can be effectively supervised only by foremen and leaders thoroughly familiar with these customs and traditions ... For example if a miner should break a dish at breakfast he will under no circumstances go into the mine that day, believing that to do so would be certain death. Locally trained supervisors understand and respect the belief; young graduates of Tokyo's giant universities are less likely to be sympathetic. To make the personnel procedures fit the realities of supervisory demands in the mine, the company has developed a system of having two persons fill each of the intermediate supervisory posts. One is an experienced man with years in the locality. The other is a young engineer who may or may not remain in the local work situation for his full career. He must at any rate leave the actual supervision of the miners to his partner.

There are many similar situations in Japan; this is merely an extreme example of a common problem. The company is caught between the quite theoretical training of the Japanese university and the social demands of recruitment in the Japanese factory which prevent the staffing of managerial posts from the ranks of the work force.[8]

As industry becomes larger and more complex the demands on management become greater. Hence, with increasing industrialization the background of managers tends to change. Professional management, selected and promoted on merit, takes the place of managers chosen by nepotism and the 'old boy' network. But this is only true in countries where the class barriers are sufficiently fluid to permit it. Even in the English-speaking world, where, according to the success literature, management is, and always has been, open to the talents, social barriers persist. Studies in the USA and the UK show that, so far at least, merit is by

8. Abegglen, James, op. cit., pp. 82–3.

T—F

no means the only qualification for getting to the top. The Acton Society study of the background of over 3,000 British managers showed that a man who had been to a public school had ten times the average chance of becoming a manager.[9] Comparisons with a study[10] of managers' backgrounds in the USA suggested that the proportion of top managers who came up from the bottom in Britain was 15 per cent and in the USA 20 per cent. 'Up from the bottom' was defined as their having no special educational qualifications, and starting their career as labourers, clerks or salesmen. In both countries the privileged entry card to top management is still often a certain type of social background; but even those with the right background increasingly need another entry card, a degree or professional qualification.

The social background of managers may be changing slowly in Britain, and the educational background more rapidly, but the kind of personality which succeeds in business has changed most of all. As we saw in the last chapter on leadership, the kind of leader needed changes with changes in the situation. The type of organization and the nature of the problems which management has to meet help to determine what sort of men will make good managers. There is less opportunity now for the enterprising individualist, particularly if he is dictatorially inclined, for the organization builder, than there is for the man who can run existing organizations. The 'organization man', the man who will ask people, rather than tell them, who can work successfully with his colleagues on decisions which must usually be arrived at in close consultation with others, who knows how to explain, persuade and, when necessary, give in gracefully, is the kind of manager who is needed to run the established industrial giants.

9. *Management Succession*, p. 8, The Trust, London, 1956.
10. Stewart, Rosemary G., and Duncan-Jones, Paul, 'Educational Background and Career History of British Managers, with some American Comparisons', *Explorations in Entrepreneurial History*, vol. IX, no. 2, pp. 61–71, December 1956.

MANAGEMENT'S ATTITUDE TO LABOUR

How managers regard their employees is reflected in management's attitude to authority on the one hand, and in the conditions of work and employee services on the other. Management's attitude to labour has changed greatly in the last fifty years in Britain and the USA. It also differs considerably from one country to another, and even, to a lesser extent, from one industry or locality to another. Management may be authoritarian – expecting unquestioning obedience to orders and without concern for the employee's welfare; authoritarian and paternalistic; constitutional – acting in accordance with the rules laid down by government, trade unions, and management; or, at least to some extent, democratic – that is, permitting employees some share in decision-making.[11]

How much authority management has, and how it exercises it, depends partly on the width of the gap which exists in class and education, between management and workers, and partly on the limitations on management's freedom of action which are imposed by government and by the trade unions. Management's authority generally declines with increasing industrialization. The standard of living rises, making the background of managers and managed more similar so that management's authority can rest less on social distance.[12] Management's authority is also restricted by the growth of government regulations and of trade union power.

11. These distinctions are based on those made by Harbison, Frederick, and Myers, Charles A., *Management in the Industrial World: An International Analysis*, ch. III, McGraw-Hill, New York, 1959.

12. 'Social distance' is the term used by sociologists to describe the extent to which individuals or groups willingly consent to share certain experiences. The smaller the social distance the more willing are they to share intimate experiences. Sociologists have measured the amount of social distance between different groups by asking people whether they would admit a particular group to close kinship by marriage, to being neighbours in the same street, etc.

The gap, or social distance, which exists between different levels in the organization reflects both the class structure in the society as a whole and management's place in it. In a very class-bound society much of management's authority may rest on social distance; whether it does so effectively will depend upon the relations which exist between management and labour. In a country which still retains some feudal traditions, management may receive the natural social deference that social inferiors give to their superiors. Where no feudal tradition remains this type of authority is likely to be strongly resented.

Nowadays the part played by government in establishing rules for employee conditions is likely to be greatest in the early stages of industrialism. Conditions in the older industrial countries set a standard by which employee treatment in the underdeveloped country can be judged, but the unions are not yet powerful enough to ensure adequate protection. So the workers turn to the government. In Latin America the government plays a very active role in industrial relations. This is, at least partly, due to the hesitations that workers, in a highly stratified society, experience in expressing their difficulties direct to management. In such a society there is a much stronger emphasis on authority and deference to the superior than in the English-speaking countries. The workers, therefore, find it easier to get somebody in a government labour department to express their grievances to management.

It should be remembered what a change there has been in Britain, as in other Western countries, in the employer's attitude to the employee. In the early days of industrialization the large majority of British employers, who might otherwise have been kind-hearted men, had no feeling of responsibility for the welfare of their employees and were only forced by the Factory Acts to provide minimal conditions for health and safety. As Croome and Hammond point out:

The new manufacturers, with a few honourable exceptions, felt no responsibility for the welfare of their workers; nor was their own self-interest enlightened enough to show them that better work can be got from well-paid, well-fed, well-housed men and women working under decent conditions for reasonable hours, than from half-starved, brutalized and exhausted workers and overdriven children. The treatment of children in the new factories was, indeed, the crowning disgrace of the Industrial Revolution. Hours in the cotton factories were anything up to sixteen a day and rarely below twelve. . . . Conditions of work were by modern standards equally appalling. . . . The workers were completely under the thumb of their 'masters and proprietors', to use the then Lord Londonderry's phrase, subject to arbitrary overtime, arbitrary punishment, arbitrary fines and deductions, and arbitrary dismissal.[13]

Even the differences in some companies between pre- and post-war are marked. What would be considered normal practice then would be looked on as inhuman today.

Once management accepts some responsibility for its employees, it may show this in several ways. It may be paternalistic, either because this is, as in Japan, a carry-over from a feudal society, or because management chooses to express its concern for its employees' welfare in that way and meets little or no opposition from them to the dependent role implicit in paternalism. Paternalistic employers are also still found in both the USA and the UK, although they are more common in countries like Italy where class divisions are stronger and where there is a master–servant, father–son relationship in industry.

Nor does paternalism necessarily vanish with advancing industrialism for in Japan, a highly industrialized country, workers are hired for life and almost never sacked.[14] There, paternalism even extends to the pay packet which is based on a variety of factors, of which the most important are the employee's educational status on entering the company and his length of service – a system of payment that obviously discourages mobility. The employee will also get a family allowance. Only a small part of his total pay will depend on

13. Croome, H. M., and Hammond, R. J., *An Economic History of Britain*, pp. 159–60, Christophers, London, revised edition, 1947.
14. Abegglen, James G., op. cit., p. 12.

the kind of work he does and the way in which he does it.[15]
He will also receive a great range of social benefits from his
company for, according to James Abegglen:

> The company is held to be and considers itself responsible for
> the total person, including his food, clothing, and shelter, and
> takes a direct responsibility for providing these things along
> with such items as medical care and education.[16]

The obligations assumed by the company when they hire a
worker even extend to the arrangement of successful mar-
riages by the manager of the plant for his female employees
before they are thirty.

Paternalistic management, according to Harbison and
Myers, is likely to be most stable:

1. when the pre-existing culture and social structure are congenial to this type of superior-subordinate relationship, as
   in Japan, India, France and Italy, and
2. when there are no strong labor organizations to challenge the
   employer's and/or manager's decisions about what should
   be done for employees. It is less stable under pressures forcing
   management to change its philosophy and approach in dealing with workers.[17]

The amount of paternalism will also be affected by the
extent to which the State provides welfare services. It can
be argued that State provision makes the worker, and the
manager, less dependent upon a paternalistic employer and,
therefore, gives him greater freedom.

Paternalism is attractive to some employers because it
makes them the giver of favours for which they expect grati-
tude, loyalty, and hard work. Such an employer is likely to
feel righteous indignation if his employees are not grateful –
'look at all I have done for them'. The paternalistic employer
may distinguish those whom he wishes to favour from the
others. Such arbitrary distribution of privileges will cause
difficulty if the company is taken over by one that has a per-

15. ibid., p. 54.
16. ibid., p. 61.
17. Harbison and Myers, op. cit., p. 58.

sonnel policy based on rules. The company, which believes in a uniform personnel policy, then, has the unenviable choice of perpetuating the arbitrary division of privileges until the individuals who benefited from it have left the company, or of establishing a uniform policy which will mean that some people may do much less well than before the merger. However, paternalism is not necessarily arbitrary; it may be associated with a well-defined personnel policy which seeks to be both fair and humane in its application.

When good employee conditions are more of a right than a favour, we have moved from paternalistic to, what Harbison and Myers have called, constitutional management. These rights may come from legislation or they may, especially in the USA, be included in the bargain which labour makes with management. Either way, they promote, as we saw in the first chapter, the growth of bureaucracy. In industry, as in society as a whole, a constitutional approach by establishing rules safeguards the individual from interference by his superiors. Such safeguards inevitably limit the power of the superiors and hence their freedom of action. As Harbison and Myers say:

The democratic-liberal nations, such as the United States of America, Great Britain, and Sweden, have this type of managerial philosophy more often than the others. Perhaps it is not a philosophy which many managers would consciously choose, if they had alternatives; but most do not have alternatives. They come increasingly to accept the fact that they must deal with the work-force under prescribed or agreed-upon rules, and they adjust their policies and behaviour to fit these conditions and limitations.[18]

Ruthless, autocratic management takes no account of employees' welfare or wishes; paternalistic management is concerned with employees' welfare but decides what it thinks is best for them; constitutional management, which may be mixed with some paternalism, treats its employees in accordance with the rules laid down by government or agreed

18. ibid., p. 62.

with the union. None of them regard their employees as partners in a democratic enterprise, although some may talk of copartnership while limiting it to profit-sharing. Finally management may genuinely regard its employees as partners in the enterprise and, therefore, entitled to participate in the decisions, at least in those directly affecting them. Rarely, such participation may extend to other aspects of company policy.

How is management likely to exercise authority in the future? There seems little to suggest that many companies will practise participative management. This requires a belief that it is right to do so (which is uncommon amongst managers and not markedly on the increase) as well as a personality that can cope with the problems inherent in any genuine attempt to encourage employees to share in some aspects of decision-making. Participative management will not work just because it is law, or because management thinks it will pay. Managers who do not genuinely believe that people have a right to share in decisions affecting them are likely to be too irritated by the difficulties which arise in discussions.

The enforced growth of constitutional management has restricted the opportunities for autocratic management. Some managers are, and always will be, more autocratic than others; but none can be nearly as autocratic as they could in the last century. Paternalism is also on the decline in the USA and UK, although it still exists and may well continue to do so in a small number of firms. Constitutional management has become, and seems likely to remain, the most common form in the USA and the UK. Personnel policy is becoming codified. The main query is whether the rules are going to be increasingly imposed on management by government and trade unions, or whether management will retain or extend its area of freedom of action.

In exercising authority managers take many things for granted. A British manager, for instance, used to a society with a long industrial history will take for granted a work-force which is adapted to industry; that is, one which expects to work regularly and to take orders about the methods and pace of work. Technology has increasingly reduced the opportunities for individuals to behave differently at work, as specialized production requires that people shall work in a prescribed manner and therefore be subject to external, rather than internal, discipline. If the British manager goes to an underdeveloped country he will find that employees are used to an agricultural society which has a different rhythm of work from an industrial society, one that gives the labourer far more control over the way in which, and the pace at which, he works. Hence, the assumptions that the manager used, to guide him in Britain, will no longer be valid. This may cause less difficulty in underdeveloped countries than in other industrial countries, like France or Italy, where the differences are smaller but may be more difficult to spot. Countries like Nigeria or Peru are so obviously different from Britain, that a manager might expect differences in employees' attitudes and be prepared to re-think some aspects of his relations with his employees. Because the relationship between management and worker varies in different countries, most companies operating in other industrial countries try, if they can, to recruit local management to deal with labour.

LABOUR'S ATTITUDE TO MANAGEMENT

The way in which management exercises its authority, and the social structure within which it does so, will largely determine labour's view of management. For instance, it should already be clear from the previous discussion that the attitude of the Japanese worker to his manager will be quite different from that of the British or American. We shall limit our discussion here to some of the reasons for differences between industries, differences which have not been relevant to the previous discussion.

Many people, including managers in strike-free companies, say that managers get the labour relations they deserve. This is only a half-truth, for it is much harder to have good industrial relations in some industries than in others. A good management may be handicapped by a legacy of bad relations in the company which may take years to live down, or by being in an industry with a long record of bad relations.

Analysis of strike figures show that some industries have a much higher incidence of strikes than others, and that this is true for the same industries in many different countries. A study of man-days lost through strikes over a number of years in eleven countries,[19] showed that, with an occasional exception, it was possible to discern a similar pattern of incidence of strikes.[20] The authors of the study attribute the differences in the propensity to strike to social reasons.

The main reason, they think, why miners and dockers in all countries have such a high propensity for striking is that they are an isolated, relatively homogeneous mass, almost a race apart, living in their own communities with their own distinctive ways of life. They share the same grievances and do similar work and have similar experiences. It is also hard to get out of this mass; the skills are specialized and not transferable. The opportunities for promotion are also limited. According to Kerr and Siegel:

The strike for this isolated mass is a kind of colonial revolt against far-removed authority, an outlet for accumulated tensions, and a substitute for occupational and social mobility.[21]

There are two other reasons they suggest for an industry to

19. Australia (1919–46), Czechoslovakia (1921–36), Germany (1915–32), Italy (1916–23), Netherlands (1918–40), New Zealand (1920–48), Norway (1925–39), Sweden (1920–37), Switzerland (1927–49), United Kingdom (1911–45), United States (1927–48). The differences in the periods studied were determined by the years for which usable figures were available.

20. Kerr, Clark, and Siegel, Abraham, 'The Interindustry Propensity to Strike – an International Comparison', *Industrial Conflict* (edited by Kornhauser, A., Dubin, R. and Ross, A. M.), McGraw-Hill, New York ,1954.

21. ibid., p. 193.

be specially strike-prone: that the group is capable of uniting – this generally results from close, continuous contact; and that the work is unpleasant and thus provides plenty of opportunities for grievances.

By contrast workers in occupations with a low strike record such as agriculture, trade, public utilities and services, are absorbed in society as a whole. They are more likely, except for farm labourers, to live in communities of different occupations and to mix with people with different experiences. Therefore, they do not have the same opportunities as the miners or dockers to share, and thus to foster, their grievances. They also usually have more opportunities of changing their work or being promoted.

This short account of industrial differences in the likelihood of strikes is one illustration of the way in which differences in social structure can affect management problems. It may perhaps make managers in relatively strike-free industries more sympathetic with the trials of their colleagues in less favourably placed industries. In the next chapter on the effects of size, we shall see another way in which management problems may be affected by the situation of the company – a situation which may be partly or even wholly outside the managers' control.

SUMMARY

Why managers think and act as they do is partly due to the type of people they are, but even more to their environment. This is made up of the social and economic history of the country in which they are working, including the stage of industrialization; the position of business in society; the prevailing moral standards; the relationship of the social classes; the strength of the trade union movement; and the number and type of government regulations. Both the methods of conducting business, and the attitudes to employees will mainly depend on what is customary at that time and place.

The educational and social background of managers varies in different countries. This is one reason why the approach of a French business man tends to be different from that of a British, and both of them different from a Japanese. In some countries the family still plays a dominant role, although its influence is declining in the USA and the UK. Even so, in both countries a man's social background still has a considerable influence on his chances of becoming a manager. The professional background of a manager can also influence his view of management. In Germany where engineers play a big role in management, the approach to business is likely to be different from Britain, where accountants are more favoured for top management.

How management exercises its authority differs over time, as well as between countries. One factor which influences it is the width of the social gap which exists between management and workers. In some countries managers still receive a feudal deference from their workers. With increasing industrialization management's authority declines, partly because a rising standard of living reduces the distance between management and workers, partly because trade unions and government regulations restrict management's freedom of action. Authoritarian management is replaced in many countries by constitutional management which manages in accordance with the rules negotiated with trade unions or laid down by the government. Paternalistic management still flourishes in countries where the class relationship is congenial to it, but it is declining in others.

Labour's attitude to management is a response to how management exercises its authority. It is also a reflection of the social structure. There are marked differences between industries as well as between countries and in the same country at different periods in its history. Some industries, for instance, have been shown to be strike-prone. The reasons are social ones. Hence, it is only partly true to say that managements get the labour relations they deserve.

9

Management in Big Business

WHAT DIFFERENCE does size make to management problems? This is the question that we are going to try to answer in this chapter. It is an important one, for, as we saw in Chapter 1, large firms form a substantial and increasing part of the economy. Some management problems become more difficult in large organizations, others are easier, while yet others are a mixture of the two. We shall not discuss all the advantages and disadvantages of bigness, because we are mainly concerned with the differences which size makes to the management of people. It will be sufficient to summarize, for the sake of perspective, the well-known advantages which are mainly financial and technical,[1] and then to examine in some detail the disadvantages which are chiefly in human relations. We shall concentrate on the disadvantages in the belief that a clearer awareness of what they are, and of what may be done to lessen them, can be helpful.

THE ADVANTAGES OF LARGE ORGANIZATIONS

The main financial and technical advantages of large companies – the reasons for many mergers and take-overs – are: the economics of large-scale production; easier access to finance; the spread of risks, including better opportunities for diversification, and the ability to undertake technical tasks which require great expenditure. The last can be a key

1. Those who are interested in a much more detailed and more economic discussion can find it in Edwards, Ronald S., and Townsend, Harry, *Business Enterprise: Its Growth and Organization*, pp. 183–93, op. cit.

reason for mergers in industries which have a heavy expenditure on research and development. Another advantage is that a large company is more powerful and therefore less likely to be taken over. Even so, size does not guarantee protection. Many of the arguments for nationalization rested on the financial and technical advantages of large-scale organization. The economic advantages of large-scale organization are so well-known that we have not elaborated on them. Yet, judging by the continual increase in the proportion of large companies they are of overriding importance.

One of the most important advantages of a large firm, according to Edwards and Townsend, is that its size enables exceptional managerial abilities to be used to the full.[2] There is, however, a corresponding disadvantage that, since managers with exceptional abilities are scarce, a large organization which does not have outstanding managers may run into difficulties. Its managers might be completely satisfactory in a smaller company but might not be able to cope successfully with the scale of problems in a large organization. It is one's estimate of the supply of exceptional managerial ability that will determine whether one agrees with Edwards and Townsend's arguments. Certainly, the anxiety shown by some of the most successful large companies about how to get good top managers suggests that the supply is too small to meet the ever-growing demands. Occasionally, outstanding men are found in medium-sized companies where their abilities may be restricted by lack of capital. Then a merger with a larger company can give them much greater scope.

The large firm usually has an advantage in recruiting staff, especially for management posts. Many people prefer to be associated with a large well-known company for its reputation – outside people will have heard of the company where they work – for its better facilities, greater security, and better opportunities for promotion to interesting and well-paid jobs. The large company is also able to spend time and money on trying to attract the people it wants. It

2. ibid., p. 183.

will have an advantage in promotion too, because it will have a bigger pool on which to draw, particularly for management posts. Although the big company has an advantage in recruitment there are people at all levels who will prefer to work for a small or medium-sized one. In the next section we shall see some of the reasons for such a preference.

THE DISADVANTAGES

The greatest problem of large-scale organization is how to prevent feelings of indifference or frustration. Junior and middle management may feel frustrated because they are a long way from effective authority and cannot get a quick decision when they need it. Workers, both manual and clerical, may feel little or no identification with the company where they work. All may miss the feeling of personal loyalty and involvement which can come from working for 'the boss'. Even the man at the top may feel frustrated because of the number of people who have to be consulted before an important decision is taken.

It is lower down the management hierarchy that feelings of frustration are most likely. These may be caused by long delays in getting a decision, by poor communication with other, related departments, and by uncertainties about the scope of one's authority. Two features of large-scale organization can be the sources of many of the difficulties: a long chain of command, and a large number of specialists. The length of the chain will depend upon the pattern of organization, if it is a 'flat' one, where a large number of managers report to one man, there may be only three links in the chain on the sales side and four or five on production; but in large organizations modelled on the span of control theory, there may be as many as twelve or more. Each additional level in the management hierarchy is a potential obstacle to communication. Each reduces the responsibility of those below, so that those at the bottom of the management ladder, or even part of the way up, may feel frustrated by the small opportunity for exercising responsibility. How serious this feeling is likely to be will depend on the extent of centralization, and on the consistency and clarity of the policies for what decisions can be taken at different levels.

The effects of a long chain of command are most likely to be harmful when it is suddenly created. The Acton Society's study of management organization under the nationalized industries showed the impact of the change to a large organization on the operational manager. That is, the manager whose main task is to take responsibility for the day-to-day operation of a production or service unit, such as a colliery or a power station.[3] Previously, the colliery manager, for instance, even in the largest companies, would see his managing director about once a week. Thus, he could put his problems to the people who really mattered. After nationalization, with several tiers between him and the national board, he could no longer do so and had scant opportunity for face-to-face contact with top management. This led to a feeling of remoteness from the effective power in the industry and to complaints of over-centralization. Nor are such feelings confined to nationalized industry, although they are likely to be greatest where, as in the nationalized industries, there is a rapid change in the amount of authority exercised by operational managers. In any large organization, junior and middle management is likely to feel that it has too little responsibility, with all the possible dangers that this may have for morale. This feeling will be more intense in a highly centralized company.

The relations between line and staff can cause difficulty in a medium-sized company, but even more in a large one. This also showed up all too clearly in the early days of nationalization, since most of the managers had little or no experience of specialists. The Acton Society's report suggested that most of the nationalized industries may have acted too quickly and on too large a scale in trying to improve technical efficiency by the use of specialists. This resulted in some of the operational managers feeling that

3. *Management Under Nationalization; Studies in Decentralization.* The Trust, London, 1953.

'they have been swamped by a torrent of specialists, who have usurped many of their most important functions'.[4] The difficulties of convincing line managers, who were unused to them, of the value of specialists was either overlooked or ignored, so that little or no effort was made to help man-agers to get used to the change. Nor was there sufficient real-ization of how long it takes to create the confidence on which a successful line-staff relationship must be based. In a long-established organization, line and staff will be used to work-ing together and can have developed mutual trust but, as we saw in Chapter 2, it is always a potentially difficult rela-tionship.

A long chain of command and a large number of special-ists make the manager's job a highly specialized one com-pared to his counterpart in a small, or medium-sized, under-taking. Hence, it is difficult for him to get experience of different functions, or to have much conception of the busi-ness as a whole. So long as he remains in middle manage-ment, this may not matter, but if he is promoted to top management he will need a wider experience and know-ledge. The difficulties of producing general managers in an organization where all, except those right at the top, are specialists, is one of the problems which worries large com-panies that are concerned about management succession. Some top managers of large companies have been known to bewail the absence of small subsidiaries, where they could give their bright young men some experience of general management. Another, related, difficulty is that some of those who might make good top managers are not prepared for the long slog in positions of little responsibility which is a prerequisite for promotion in many large companies, especially in those with a many-tiered hierarchy. Hence, some keen young men will opt for smaller companies, where they can make a mark more quickly and get a wide exper-ience of management which will be useful later if they want to move.

A feeling amongst junior and lower-middle managers

4. ibid., p. 68.

that they are far removed from effective authority is one of the dangers of large organizations. This feeling can be more pronounced on the shop-floor, which may be faced with a local management which does not have the authority to give a decision on a question raised by the union, or by the workers' representatives on the joint consultative committee. Again, this problem was specially acute in the early days of nationalization. The workers, who previously had soon got a yes or no from management, now found that a subject raised in the consultative, or in the negotiating, machinery often had to be referred upwards. The delay in either might be well over a year. As one trade union official put it, 'If you go through the proper channels there will be a delay of months if not longer, but if you have even a small strike, the Chairman and Chief Industrial Relations Officer will be on the spot within twenty-four hours.' At least the workers have a way of quickly getting to top management, a way which is not open to the frustrated operational manager.

The most frequently mentioned problem of large organizations is not the frustrations of lower management, but the difficulties of creating or maintaining good management-worker relations. The interest in incentives, and in ways of encouraging greater management-worker cooperation, all stem from the divorce between the two which develops as a firm grows larger. In the smallest firm, such as a small builder and decorator, the workers may identify themselves with the business. As it grows from 5 employees to 50, from 50 to 100 and from 100 to 500, there will be changes in the relationship between the boss and his employees, even if 'the boss' remains the same. Above about 600 employees no manager can really know all his employees, however gifted his abilities to do so; hence, that form of personal touch and personal knowledge comes to an end. The employee's feeling of personal responsibility for the success of the company diminishes as the company grows: whether he is late or absent becomes a purely personal question that may be affected by penalties for bad timekeeping rather than by a concern for any disruption he may cause.

The size of the organization may, depending upon the way in which it is organized and how it has grown, have an important effect on the morale of the junior and middle managers. The size of the establishment, that is the individual producing unit, whether factory, colliery, power station or retail store, is more important in its effects on workers' morale than the size of the company as a whole. An Acton Society study tried to assess workers' morale – the level of enthusiasm for work – by comparing the amount of time people took off work.[5] The assumption made was that if people's morale was high they would take less time off work than if it was low. The study compared the lost-time rates in different sized establishments: in the coal industry, in a large retail chain-store, and in a manufacturing company. In all three, absenteeism was higher in the larger units. A follow-up study, in one organization with different sized establishments, all producing the same thing, attempted to find the reasons for this relationship between size and lost-time rates.[6] The organization in the second study had a similar relationship, but a more detailed analysis showed that within the general trend, there were some small units with higher lost-time rates than some of the large ones. There seemed to be three explanations for the higher lost-time rates. One, that the large establishments had special disadvantages: a higher rate of cross-infection and more employees with bad sickness and lateness records. These were not employed in the small units as their absences would be too disruptive. In an organization that transferred employees with high sickness records to the larger units, this could be an important factor in relative sickness rates. A private study in another company showed that a small proportion of chronic sick accounted for a much higher than average amount of absences.[7] Two, that the

5. *Size and Morale*, The Trust, London, 1953.
6. Acton Society Trust, *Size and Morale II*. The Trust, London, 1957.
7. cf. Acton Society Trust, *Retirement*, p. 53, The Trust, London, 1960.

small units had a much smaller span of control at the foreman level than the large units, so that the foreman's opportunity to know his men and their problems was better.
Three, that a higher calibre of management was necessary
in the larger units to help overcome the anonymity of size;
the higher quality of management seemed to be the explanation for the few, large units which diverged from the
trend to higher lost-time rates.

Other reactions of employees to working in large establishments can be seen in strikes and in accidents. Strikes are
more common in large coal-mines. In the Yorkshire coal-
field, according to Professor Revans, the average miner in
the average pit with less than 500 workers loses a shift a year
in disputes; in pits with between 500 and 1,000 he loses three
shifts a year. The number of lost shifts increases until it
is six a year in pits with over 2,500 men.[8] A similar reaction to size can be seen in a different form of organization
– hospitals. Statistics of 837,000 hospital workers employed
in 4,360 American hospitals in 1953 showed a steady increase in the mean accident-rate with the size of hospital.
The rate, for all accidents causing absence other than on the
day of the accident, was more than five times as great in a
hospital with over 2,000 workers as it was in a hospital with
less than 20.[9] This size-effect can also be found in the working
group itself. According to Revans, 'it is not only the total
size of the coal-mine that influences the willingness of men
to cooperate; this willingness is also markedly determined by
the average size of the groups within the mine in which men
work'.[10]

So far we have not mentioned what are traditionally supposed to be the disadvantages of large organizations: inflexibility, red-tape, and empire-building. Obviously these
are all well-known temptations – to judge only by the roar of

8. Revans, R. W., 'Is Work Worthwhile?' *Personnel Management*,
vol. XL, no. 343, pp. 12–21, Institute of Personnel Management,
London, March 1958.

9. ibid., p. 17.

10. ibid.

approval that greeted *Parkinson's Law*. The amount of paper must go up as a company grows and artificial eyes and ears have to be substituted for personal knowledge and word of mouth. Both the amount of paper and the rate of empire-building may be increased if managers feel insecure; they may commit everything to paper to protect themselves, or build empires to bolster their prestige. In our chapter on bureaucracy we saw that the characteristics of bureaucracy may be developed to extremes. Like many good things they can be overdone. Rules are necessary, but there is always a temptation to add to them. Yet the dangers of red-tape and empire-building in large organizations can be held in check.

A more difficult problem is inflexibility and delay. The process of working out the general aims of the organization, getting agreement for changes, keeping each part of the organization informed, and checking it if it departs from the common aims and plan, is a laborious one. There may be so many people to be consulted before an important decision is made that it can take much longer in a large company than in a medium-sized one. As long ago as 1925, Alfred E. Sloan, chairman of General Motors, bemoaned that:

In practically all our activities we seem to suffer from the inertia resulting from our great size. It seems to be hard for us to get action when it comes to a matter of putting our ideas across. There are so many people involved and it requires such a tremendous effort to put something new into effect, that a new idea is likely to be considered insignificant in comparison with the effort that it takes to put it across.

... Sometimes I am almost forced to the conclusion that General Motors is so large that it is impossible for us to really be leaders.[11]

Nor are the problems of inertia likely to be much different in the large companies of the 1960s. All of them have to cope

11. From a speech to General Motors' sales committee, July 29, 1925, quoted by the Temporary National Economic Committee, *Relative Efficiency of Large, Medium-Sized and Small Business*, Monograph 13, pp. 130–31, US Government Printing Office, Washington, 1941.

with the fact that the amount of energy required to oppose is much less than that required to initiate and carry through a change. How much inertia and resistance there will be depends partly upon the background and calibre of the people recruited, partly on the atmosphere within the company and partly on how used its managers are to change.

DIFFERENT WAYS OF BEING BIG

So far we have talked about the problems of large-scale organization as if they were common to all large companies. So indeed they are, but their intensity will vary according to how the firm has grown, how it is organized, and what stage it has reached in its history. Organizations can become big in different ways: they can grow gradually like Shell Petroleum or with greater rapidity like the Atomic Energy Authority; they can be created like ICI, by the amalgamation of a small number of fair-sized companies, or, in exceptional circumstances, they can become big overnight as when 800 companies were changed into the National Coal Board. The faster the rate of growth the greater will be the problems, that is why the early days of the nationalized industries have been used for a number of the illustrations.

The rate of growth intensifies management problems of coordination and human relations because tradition can play little or no part. Much of the work of a company, as we saw in the chapter on 'People and Organization', is carried out through informal contact. But in a company created by amalgamation, there will be no common 'old-boy' network and its growth will inevitably take time. A lengthy mutual process of getting to know one another, both in terms of recognition and of assessment, will have to go on. In some ways a company which expands very rapidly has fewer problems than one that is created by amalgamations, or grows through mergers, because it will have a core of people who know each other on which to build. In other ways it can be more difficult, because the changes that have to be made may be less obvious than they are in an amalgamation.

Companies may continue to grow by mergers as well as by expansion of existing resources. Any merger creates problems of how to fit the new company into the existing structure. The parent, unless it is only a financial holding company, will seek, to a greater or lesser extent, to mould the new acquisition to the parental pattern. The technical, financial, and administrative changes may amount to almost complete integration or only to control of selected aspects of the business. In theory these changes need not take long but, if the management of the parent company is anxious not to kill the growing tree in the process, not to destroy management initiative and enthusiasm, they will have to be made slowly. Unless it is a relatively small acquisition the parent company may also gradually change during the process of adjustment. Hence the necessity, underlined by a number of companies with experience of mergers, for allowing sufficient time for digestion before embarking on a new merger.

Whatever the difficulties for management created by large-scale organization, they do not prevent large firms from growing still larger, or the number of large firms from increasing. The financial and technical advantages of size are usually sufficient to outweigh the disadvantages. The study mentioned earlier of the 100 largest British companies in terms of net assets showed that from 1949 to 1953, the period covered by the study, these companies expanded at a faster rate than the other 2,800 manufacturing and distributing companies quoted on the Stock Exchange; their profits grew at a compound rate of 12 per cent a year compared to 8 per cent for the other companies.[12] Since large companies form an ever-increasing share of the economy, it is important that we should examine what can be done to reduce their disadvantages, and especially their disadvantages for the employee, whether manager or worker.

12. Prais, S. J., op. cit., p. 257.

WHAT CAN BE DONE?

The list of disadvantages of large-scale organizations has been a long one: a many-tiered management structure, with its dangers of poor communication and a feeling of remoteness from effective authority; junior and middle managers who feel that they do not have enough responsibility; line managers who feel their authority is threatened by specialists; specialists who feel frustrated because their advice is not taken; workers who feel their contribution does not matter and who become indifferent to the success of the company; inflexibility, form-filling, and empire-building. Yet even then the list is not exhaustive. These are dangers inherent in large-scale organizations, but they can all be mitigated if not avoided. They are problems which may have to be lived with, but which can be kept in check by awareness and watchfulness. As we saw in the study of size of unit and lost-time rates, there were large units which did not follow the trend to higher lost-time rates. Similarly, there are large companies with excellent labour relations.

Much can be done, by the philosophy and policies of management and by changes in the organization structure, to reduce the human disadvantages of bigness. In the list of disadvantages in the previous paragraph the word 'feel' recurs. People in large organizations can more easily *feel* unimportant, insecure and, if they are managers or foremen, uncertain of their authority or prospects. A management which really believes that people are individuals, and that individuals matter, can constantly seek to give effect to this belief. It may, for instance, experiment with increasing the content of jobs if it thinks that people find their jobs too narrow. It can try to promote those who share its belief in the importance of individuals.

One of the ways in which the anonymity of top management – with all its possible implications of a lack of feeling – may be lessened, even in the largest company, is by the actions of the managing director. If he really cares about individuals, and is able to make this public knowledge, it can influence the attitudes of employees at all levels. This was strikingly shown in one company where the managing director not merely cared deeply about the welfare of his employees, but wrote and broadcast about his philosophy of management so that many of his employees had heard of it. He also made a point of visiting any newly-acquired company and meeting many of its employees. The result was that a number of the managers in these companies, when interviewed about their reactions to the merger, said that they felt they could go to the managing director if they had a complaint and get a fair deal. Another managing director said that he regarded his appearances on television as one way of being known to his employees.

Much can also be done by the form of the organization to prevent people from feeling frustrated. Since we saw that the size of working groups, and the size of establishments are related to such indices of morale as absenteeism, accidents and strikes. Hence, a company which has small working groups and small establishments will tend to have fewer problems with worker-morale and cooperation, than companies with large establishments and large working groups. The nature of its business will determine what choice it has in this aspect of its organization, but at least managers should be aware of the importance of any element of choice there may be.

Good human relations require more conscious thought and effort in a large organization than in a small one where the right attitude can take a manager much further. In a large organization a manager needs a greater understanding of the possible sources of frustration, as he may not see the symptoms of frustration until they show in lost-time rates, high labour turnover, strikes and management-ulcers. A manager who remembers, for instance, that a long delay in getting a decision, uncertainty about the scope of one's authority, or the views of one's superior, can be frustrating will take more trouble to avoid these than an equally well-intentioned manager who does not.

Many problems are intensified in a highly centralized organization, which encourages red-tape and resistance to change and which gives the more junior managers little opportunity to exercise responsibility. Therefore, an important organizational aim is to centralize as little as possible and to keep the number of tiers in the management hierarchy to the minimum. But the 'as possible' is important. What is possible, as we saw in Chapter 2, will vary at different periods in a company's history. More centralization, for instance, was necessary in the early days of nationalization, as in many other forms of amalgamation.

How much decentralization is possible will also vary in different industries; the opportunities for it are obviously less in the mass production of cars, or in steel-making, than in industries where production can economically be broken down into separate units. Some companies are inescapably committed to large establishments which, as we saw earlier, are probably more important factors in morale than the overall size of the company. Others may have some choice both in the size of their establishments and in whether they divide their company – as so many successful large companies are divided – into semi-autonomous subsidiaries or divisions. If it is possible to judge the profitability of a subsidiary, it is easier to go further in decentralization as it then can be treated in many ways as a separate economic unit.

The minimum of centralization that is customary in a large company is financial control over capital expenditure above a stated figure; approval of financial budgets; controls over top-level appointments and remunerations; and, probably, the conduct of national trade union negotiations. There may also be a staff of specialists at headquarters, although a number of companies limit their head office to the staff necessary to operate these central controls. According to Edwards and Townsend:

Provided one decides rightly which types of decisions to allow to come to the centre there is no reason why the problem of coordination should make a large firm less efficient than two or more smaller, independent firms. This does not mean that no large firms will suffer from unwieldiness, wooliness and slowness; but if they do so it will be because of deficiencies in particular managements, not because of the inevitable deficiencies of large organizations. Small firms may equally suffer from deficiencies in management and very frequently do.

There is no stage at which an organization must become *less* efficient than it would be if it were smaller; but beyond the point where economies of large outputs and cost-reducing advantages of large organizations are exhausted it will not be *more* efficient.[18]

It is arguable whether good organization, meaning, especially here, the right balance between centralization and decentralization, can overcome all the disadvantages of coordination in large organization as Edwards and Townsend claim. The problem of the number of people to be consulted must still remain, so must that of keeping all parts of the organization informed when necessary. That large firms can be efficient and small firms inefficient is clear, but to manage a large company as efficiently as a small one requires a high calibre of management.

SUMMARY

The continued growth in the number and size of large companies shows that economically their advantages outweigh their disadvantages – though the sceptic may say that the ability of the large fish to swallow the small is no reflection on the efficient functioning of the latter. Despite its economic advantages, a large organization has inherent difficulties which its managers must combat. To do so successfully requires better managers than in a smaller company. The large company is fortunate in being in a stronger position for recruiting such men.

One of the greatest problems of large-scale organization is how to prevent feelings of indifference or frustration. The workers may feel that their contribution does not matter and that nobody cares about them. They will find it hard to identify with the success of the company. The managers

13. Edwards and Townsend, op. cit., p. 195.

may be frustrated because of delays in getting a decision, or because of poor communication. They may feel that they do not have enough responsibility; in part, because of the number of tiers in the management structure, and in part, because they may feel plagued by specialists. Promotion is usually slower, and it is harder for managers to get experience for top management when middle-management posts are highly specialized.

As an organization grows larger the gap between management and worker widens. Various studies of the effects of size show that the larger the number employed in an establishment, the lower is morale, as measured by lost-time rates, strikes and accidents. One study suggested that although this is the general trend, there are large units which, by virtue of their good management, do not conform to it.

The traditional temptations of large-scale organization are inflexibility, red-tape, and empire-building. These dangers can be kept in check, although never abolished. But the inertia level of large organizations may always be higher than that of the efficient small company.

Although there are common problems of bigness, they will be more intense in some companies than others. It depends how the company has become big. If it has grown rapidly, whether by amalgamation or natural expansion, its problems will be greater than those of a company which has grown gradually, building on, and developing its tradition as it went. The greatest problems were found in the nationalized industries, as they became big overnight.

It is obvious that some large companies keep many of these problems under control. Their management philosophy and policies help to prevent people feeling unimportant, insecure, and frustrated. In a few, the managing director's obvious personal concern for his staff can do much to reassure them that 'the boss' does care. The type of organization can also help to prevent a feeling of remoteness; as far as possible, there should be small groups, small establishments, and a decentralized organization.

10

The Manager and Change

IN THE LAST CHAPTER we discussed some of the management problems of large organizations, but size is only one of the factors that determine the complexity of the manager's job. The amount of competition, the rapidity of change, the degree of uncertainty and of risk, as well as the particular problems of declining industries, all will help to determine how hard his life is likely to be. The top manager in a whisky distilling company, where the major change for several years may be a redesign of the label, will usually lead a more restful life than the top manager in a technical frontiers industry like electronics, or one subject to fashion changes such as the clothing industry. The would-be manager who wants an uneventful life – and there are such in all occupations – would be wise to go into a monopoly, preferably with a product with a stable market.

The greatest of all problems for the manager is rapid change, therefore this last chapter will be devoted to the impact of change on his job. How British managers react to change will have an important influence on Britain's economic future. The tempo of change has speeded up, hence the demands made on managers to plan for, and adjust to, change are greater. All change requires both abilities. Some changes can be planned for in great detail, for instance, the switch to a new model. Others may be unforeseeable but, if the organization is kept sufficiently flexible, it will be able to cope with the unexpected. The number of completely unexpected changes can be kept to a minimum by foresight. Changes also mean adjustment. Without it the planning will be unsuccessful. Adjustment is usually more difficult for the manager than planning because it has an emotional aspect to it, both for him and for his staff. He has to be able to acclimatize both himself and his subordinates to the change. The sources of major change affecting management are:

1. Innovations, which lead to new products and new methods of manufacture.
2. Shifts in market patterns as a result of innovations, of changes in consumer wants and of new methods of selling.
3. Greater competition, especially as a result of lower tariffs.
4. Changes in government regulations and taxation.
5. New tools of management, such as the computer.
6. Changes in the background, training and occupation of those employed.

Let us now look at each of these in turn to see what management can do to plan for them.

PLANNING FOR CHANGE

Innovations

The tempo of innovation is much greater than before, hence in some industries a company must spend heavily on research and development if it is to survive. To avoid stagnation or decline it must ever be on the look-out for new possibilities for growth. A study by the Stanford Research Institute of the causes of company growth[14] in the USA reported findings which can also be helpful to British management. It found that the companies which had grown most, had the following characteristics:

a. Early development of new, or rapidly growing, products and markets.
b. Organized programmes to seek and promote new business opportunities, for instance, long-range company planning, products research and development, market research, and the acquisition of other companies.

14. The companies studied were those manufacturing companies, listed in *Moody's Industrials*, an American company reference book, which from 1939 to 1949 had an increase in sales of at least 400 per cent. The sales history of these companies was also followed from 1949 to 1956. They were compared with companies which had a low rate of sales increase.

c. Proven competitive abilities in the company's present lines of business.

d. Courageous and energetic management which is willing to take carefully studied risks.

e. Good luck.[15]

The SRI study also showed that the leading areas of growth change within a few years. Hence, one of the important problems for management in a rapidly changing industry is to make certain that it is producing the right things and that it does not go on producing them for too long.

Diversification into other industries, and into other parts of the same industry, is the fashionable answer to the need to protect the company from a decline in its products. There is a danger, however, that a company may diversify without sufficient study of what products and markets are likely to grow, and of which ones are suitable for the company – suitable in terms of its capital location, access to raw materials, and managerial know-how. In diversification by merger the latter will be enlarged by the experience of the managers in the other company, thus providing a solution to the problem of inadequate managerial know-how in the chosen field.

Innovation is a lengthy business, so the company will have to plan well ahead. In selecting a research project it will have to judge the following: the likelihood of success; the time it will take; its cost and its value – judged by the likely market gain and by the need for a new or improved product. The latter will mainly depend on the competitive position and the rate of obsolescence of existing products. Completing the research project, and deciding to manufacture a new product, are only the first stages in launching a new product. The Acton Society's study of 'Management Initiative' suggested that managements may be stronger at one stage of the process of initiative than at another.[16] They may, for

15. Smith, Robert W., 'Management Implications of the SRI Study', Proceedings 3rd Annual Industrial Economic Conference, 'How Companies Grow', pp. 86–7, Stanford Research Institute, California, 1958.

16. *Management Initiative*, op. cit.

instance, be better at analysing a problem and reaching a decision than they are at getting sufficient agreement to make the implementation successful. Or they may get into difficulties at the implementation stage, because top management considers speed synonymous with efficiency and therefore tends to skimp the preliminary stages.[17] The launching of a new product may also come to grief because of the way in which it is marketed. Selling a new product may mean entering a new market and competing against those familiar with it. Curiously, some companies plan the design and manufacture of a new product with great care, but treat the marketing of it as if it was a routine matter, although the market they are entering may need quite different methods from their customary ones. They may also attach too much importance to the goodwill their name has earned elsewhere, but which may have little value in a new market where others are already established.

The chances of future success would be greater if companies more often analysed the causes of their failure. The study of 'Management Initiative' suggests that it is useful to find out at what stage the project ran into difficulties. This may show up a recurrent weakness at a particular stage. Unfortunately, management is often chary of analysing the causes of failure, either because it will not face up to the fact of failure, or because it is afraid of upsetting people.

Changes in Consumer Expenditure

The pattern of consumer expenditure is changing rapidly. The age of marriage, the average number of children and how soon after marriage they are born, the proportion of women working, the level of education, the amount of leisure, and the availability of goods, all have changed in recent years and all influence what consumers buy and when. A major factor determining how money is spent is the standard of living and how it is distributed. There is a new market, for instance, created by the high earnings of teenagers

17. ibid.

who are spending heavily on leisure goods and services, such as pop records and dance-halls.

Consumption in Great Britain increased 20 per cent in real terms – that is, adjusted for inflation – between 1948–50 and 1957–9. The way in which consumers spent their income changed radically, partly as a result of the disappearance of wartime shortages, partly because of the greater margin of surplus above necessities and partly because of a change in outlook.[18] The rising standard of living increased the proportion of money spent on 'middle-class' goods. Expenditure on private motoring shot up by 27.6 per cent; beer dropped by 1 per cent, but other alcohol went up by 43 per cent; foreign travel increased by 63 per cent and household goods by 50 per cent. Apart from the tiny fall in beer, the only two items to decrease were domestic service which fell by 41 per cent and entertainment which went down by 20 per cent. The amount of house space, hence the expenditure on housing, went up; the total available supply of dwellings increased by almost 20 per cent from 1949 to 1958, while the total population went up by only 3 per cent. The pattern of food expenditure also changed; fewer of the cheap 'filler' foods such as bread, potatoes and jam were bought and more of the expensive foods like meat and fruit. More money was also spent on food services such as preparation and wrapping – to judge by American experience much more is likely to be spent in future.

Dr Abrams suggests that:

These changes in total income and income distribution have two outstanding implications. The first is that within top management the balance of power will certainly move increasingly from the technicians and engineers to the marketing and publicity experts. The second implication is that the safest working principle for almost every producer from now on is to trade up[19] in the quality and design of his product.[20]

18. The information in this paragraph was taken from Abrams, Dr Mark, 'The Changing Pattern of Consumer Spending', *The Manager*, pp. 261–5, British Institute of Management, London, April 1960.

19. i.e., to improve.

20. ibid., p. 265.

The company which correctly foresees future consumer wants can get into a growing market at the beginning. It might take Dr Mark Abrams as a general guide when he suggests that the manufacturer of consumer comforts 'can operate on the safe principle that today's affluent consumer is tomorrow's average consumer,[21] though he should check on how many other manufacturers are acting on the same principle.

Increasing Competition

The greatest change on the horizon for much of British management is the development of the European Common Market, whether or not Britain eventually joins. Some British managements had started studying what effect it would have on them if Britain did; some have opened factories in Common Market countries to make certain of access to the market there. Unfortunately, others who are probably the majority, are like the leading British industrialist who was reported not even to know the names of his two leading Continental competitors.[22]

The managements of some British companies will be relieved that the threat of greater European competition has, at least for the time being, receded. Others will regret the opportunities they hoped to enjoy in the wider market, and may seek to compensate for them by opening more plants in Common Market countries. Yet, the implications of the Common Market must still be of concern to many British companies. Whether Britain remains permanently excluded or not, British managements will have to devote more thought and energy in order to increase, perhaps now even to retain, their present exports to the Common Market. In the struggle that lies ahead they should remember that British exporters are criticized for failing to study the overseas market sufficiently.

21. ibid., p. 265.
22. Brittan, Samuel, 'Can We Compete in Europe?', *The Observer*, London, 5 November 1961.

Changes in Government Regulations

These changes attract most attention. Unfortunately they are often unpredictable as well as being outside the control of the company. Some industries are particularly vulnerable to alterations in purchase tax and in hire-purchase restrictions which can lead to drastic reductions in the volume of sales. The adjustments for companies in such industries are bound to be severe, but something can be done to prepare for their possibility. A planned employment policy may be able to provide for some of the labour force in peak periods to consist of part-time married women or retired employees and a redundancy policy can be agreed with the unions for use if necessary. Some companies may also seek to mitigate the severity of the adjustments by diversification to products which will not be affected in the same way.

Management Tools

The number and complexity of management tools is increasing. Today many managers need to understand the contributions that 'information technology' can make to the solution of some of their problems. 'Information technology' is a general term that includes operational research, cybernetics, and the use of computers both for processing information and to simulate higher-order thinking. All these can help the manager either by providing him with much more precise information about some of his problems or by giving him information faster. Information technology may radically change the nature of middle- and top-management jobs. Leavitt and Whisler, writing in the *Harvard Business Review* in 1958, argued that it would:

1. Move the boundary between planning and performance upward, so that many middle-management jobs would lose much of their discretionary elements as operating decisions were laid down governing day-to-day decisions.
2. Lead to a recentralization in large companies as top managers will take on even more of the planning and innovating functions.
3. Result in a reorganization of middle management with some jobs moving downwards in pay and prestige because they

will require less discretion and skill, and others moving upwards into top management, because, like research and
development, they become of increasing importance.
4. Make for a sharper line between top and middle management and one which is difficult to pass.[23]

It is too early to say how far this crystal-gazing into management's future will prove to be correct, but we can already
see the decline in autonomy in some management jobs.
The factory manager in some companies, for instance, is
much less important than he used to be, as what the factory
will produce, in what quantities, and when may be decided
by head office. This tendency to reduce the responsibilities of
some middle-management jobs will be accentuated as more
of the discretionary elements in a manager's job are made
unnecessary by better information. What seems more
doubtful is whether there will be a promotion barrier between middle and top management, as the bulk of top managers are likely to continue to be recruited from middle
management.

One reason given by Leavitt and Whisler for believing
that information technology will lead to greater centralization is that it will make it much easier. They suggest that
decentralization exists for the negative reason that top
management could not adequately control large, complex
organizations, but that the new techniques will enable them
to do so. If they do, some top managers will opt for a return
to centralization. Others may still believe that decentralization is preferable on the grounds that it provides a training-
ground for future managers, a stimulant to initiative, and
a means of combating the morale problems of size.

Changes in the Composition of the Working Force
Innovation, which is increasingly essential for many companies, will lead to a higher proportion of managers and
specialists. The management ratio, that is, the proportion of

23. Leavitt, Harold, and Whisler, Thomas L., 'Management in the
1980s', *Harvard Business Review*, vol. 36, no. 6, pp. 41–2, November–
December 1958.

management staff including specialists, to total employees, varies greatly between companies of the same size. Part of this difference is due to the number of staff employed in research and development. A study of the changing employment structure of fifty American companies since World War II shows that the largest increase in the proportion of senior staff took place in the firms which were making the greatest number of changes. The firms that were innovating least showed almost no increase.[24] The management ratio is also likely to increase with greater mechanization.

By the end of the 1960s, in business as a whole, the relative proportion of managerial, professional and technical people, that is, the knowledge workers, as distinct from the manual and clerical workers, will account for the bulk of wages and salaries in American business.[25] This means that the education, occupation and outlook of the people that managers will be working with, whether as subordinates or colleagues, is changing. Hence, as Drucker suggests, 'Effective personnel management of the knowledge worker may require as much study as has been devoted in the past twenty-five years to the personnel management of the manual and clerical worker.' There is already an awareness of this need to judge by the number of studies and symposiums which have recently been published on management of the research worker.

RESISTANCES TO CHANGE

There are two main problems in the successful implementation of change: that the adjustments that are necessary may not be recognized, or that they may be resisted. Good planning will help to prevent the first but, if the change is to be

24. Hill, Samuel E., and Harbison, Frederick, 'Manpower and Innovation in American Industry', Industrial Relations Section, Princeton University, 1959, quoted in Harbison and Myers, op. cit., pp. 26–7.

25. Drucker, Peter F., 'The Next Decade in Management', Dun's Review of Modern Industry, vol. 74, no. 6, pp. 52–3 and 57–61, London, December 1959.

successful, people at all levels in the company must make the necessary adjustments, and make them in time to avoid costly delays. A knowledge of the most common causes of resistance to change can be helpful for appreciating what opposition is likely to be met and why. We shall, therefore, discuss these before turning to what can be done to ease adjustments to change.

An important source of resistance to change comes from social barriers. These, just because they are social, vary from one country to another and even from one locality or one industry to another. Many of them in Britain stem from a rigid, occupational structure which has developed mainly as a result of union pressure. (Social barriers between occupations are not, however, necessarily the result of union action, they may as in India come from the class system.) Some unions, especially craft unions, have developed rules, which are often very rigid, governing the work which is to be done by their members. These may restrict the right of entry to the union, therefore, often to the occupation, in terms of numbers, length and type of training, and sometimes to who is eligible. Such rules exist to protect union members from a lowering of their value by a dilution of standards, an increase in numbers, or an invasion of their type of work by members of another union; therefore, the bitter demarcation fights in the shipbuilding industry, and the division in the building industry as to what is a carpenter's job and what an electrician's. Hence, also, the rules governing length of apprenticeship and, in some trades, such as printing, the number of apprentices which may be admitted each year. An extreme example of restriction are the dock workers in at least one declining American port who limit new members to one son of a deceased member – 'let us hope the old man dies quickly!'

The place of one occupation in relation to others, in terms of remuneration, perks and prestige, may become established over the years. Rapid change frequently means a shift in the relative importance of occupations, the creation of new ones and the decline or even abolition of some old ones. Workers may resist a change because it affects their relative positions *vis-à-vis* other occupations, although in absolute terms they are no worse off. In recent years in Britain, changes that affected differentials between occupations aroused the fiercest reactions, because they threatened a particular group of workers' long-established ideas of their place in society.

Workers are likely to fight tenaciously for the survival of their occupation even if it has lost its *raison d'être*. A recent example is the strong opposition by the railway firemen in several countries to proposals to abolish their jobs in diesel trains where there are no fires to tend. The opposition existed despite guarantees for the protection of their livelihood. Resistance is often intensified, as in this case, by the threat that the change may affect the power of the union concerned, which may see a source of recruitment drying up, or even its own disappearance.

The manager may be impatient with occupational resistance to change. He may think that the protective rules on admission to a craft create an artificial scarcity value; that apprenticeship training is much longer than is necessary, and that the rules about who does what work are often cumbersome and restrict productivity. He may also feel that in a changing society the relative importance of different occupations is bound to change; and that this is just something that people must adjust to. In particular, he may feel that if workers are protected from economic loss they have no cause to complain; those who do are being unreasonable. In sum, he may be impatient – even furiously so – at such outmoded rules getting in the way of maximum productivity. But impatience is likely to do harm, especially if it makes him forget that much resistance to change is based on very solid reasons from the point of view of the affected individuals.

One of the most disturbing changes for an individual is that which reduces the value of his training and experience. This can happen when his skill is replaced through mechanization or innovation, or when theoretical knowledge becomes more important than experience on the job. A man may suffer economically through redundancy or lower earnings, or he may be economically protected but moved to a job which demands less skill and which has a lower prestige. He may, particularly at the supervisory and managerial levels, remain in the same job but see his chances of promotion reduced by a change in the requirements for management jobs, usually by a greater emphasis on the value of theoretical training. This is happening now to some of the managers who have come up the hard way in the steel industry and see more of the management posts being filled by metallurgists and graduate engineers. Any change which reduces the value of a man's training and experience is likely to affect his sense of personal worth and his idea of his place in the company and in society. 'Tread softly because you tread on my dreams' might be amended, as a guide to those introducing change, to, 'Tread softly because you tread on my sense of personal worth'.

Resistance to change is often closely bound up with ideas of status. The status of people at any level may be threatened by change: the craftsman may become de-skilled; the foreman may lose, indeed often already has lost, much of his authority; and the manager, who has come up the hard way, may have lower prestige than the graduate manager. Change may threaten status in two ways: by moving a man to a position of lower status; and by lowering the status of his present job. The latter often happens in some mergers where the distance from 'the boss' becomes greater. As we saw in the discussion of coal nationalization a manager who is used to reporting to the managing director may feel a considerable loss of status if he then has to report to an intermediary manager.

Another social barrier to change is the attitude to mobility which depends, in part, on the strength of local roots. The workers in some countries are more willing to move their homes than those in others. The Acton Society's case studies on redundancy suggested that British workers may be willing to change their occupation, even to take a job of lower skill or less pay, but are often very reluctant to change their locality.[26] This was a limited study, but other evidence seems to confirm the reluctance of the British worker, along with the Belgian, Italian, and Swedish, to move his home; a reluctance which may well be socially, if not economically, desirable. How reluctant he is may depend upon whether his identification with his neighbourhood is greater than his attachment to the firm. There are British companies that moved to new towns and successfuly persuaded a high proportion of their employees to accompany them, though they could have found jobs had they stayed put.

The worker may place a high value on his social relations both in the neighbourhood and at work. Changes which affect these may be resisted. A change to a shift system will have a profound effect on his life outside work and may be disliked in consequence. His social relations at work may be upset by changing the people with whom he is used to working, by altering the size of the working group or the relations with his boss. In the chapter on 'People and Organization' we saw that different types of work-organization can encourage or discourage friendly relations between members of the working groups, thus affecting job satisfaction.

Resistance to change will be intensified by fear. This will come from two sources: the realistic fears for his security which an employee at any level, who has invested the best years of his life in a company, is bound to feel; and his personal anxieties which may not be fully conscious and are aroused by anything that can be interpreted as a threat. The latter, especially, may account for the fact that even changes that improve his earnings and conditions may be viewed, at least initially, with suspicion and fear.

HELPING ADJUSTMENT TO CHANGE

Change, especially rapid change, is often upsetting.

26. *Redundancy: Three Studies on Redundant Workers*, The Trust, London, 1959.

management must recognize this if it is to ease adjustment to change. Even in changes which will be beneficial from the worker's point of view, there will be a period, while he is changing his habits, when he will have to expend more physical and emotional energy than usual. Some research in America on perceived work pressure suggests that when this goes up, as it will during a change which involves adapting to new methods of work, it affects workers' attitudes and leads to a drop in morale. At the least, change disturbs people's customary ways of doing things which may make them fearful of what is going to happen to them. At the worst it deprives them of their livelihood and destroys the value of their years of training and experience. Thus, change is often painful and may cause social casualties. It is likely to be resisted, especially if it affects people's livelihood and way of life. But there is now enough evidence from experience and research to show that the pains of change can be reduced and that resistance may be overcome or prevented if enough trouble is taken.

The human aspects of change need as careful planning as the engineering or financial. Planning should cover both the likely human effects of the change and what can be done to lessen those that are harmful. The effects may include a decrease in the number of workers needed, a change in the type of jobs to be done, a change in the method of payment, a drop in incentive earnings during the retraining period, a change in the size and make-up of the working group, and a drop in the status of some employees. Change may also impose different demands and strains on the management organization. It may even extend its effects to the social life of the community, for instance if shift work is introduced. A different kind of effect is likely to be fear; fear of what is going to happen and how it is likely to affect the individual. The planning should include a study of how a drop in the number of employees can, as far as possible, be achieved without redundancy, careful plans for retraining which are adapted to the needs of different employees, and protection against a drop in earnings during the retraining period. It should also include care in the organization of the working groups to give their members as much social satisfaction as production considerations will permit, and provisions to cushion the loss of status. For instance, long-service employees, who are likely to be the worst affected, might be given staff status. Some changes, such as shift work, are far-reaching in their effects and less can be done to reduce their impact, but even so the system adopted should be the one that is least physically and socially upsetting. The timing and method of announcing the changes should also be well-planned. Everything possible should be done to reduce the fear which comes from uncertainty and misapprehension.

One suggestion for planning, that of care in the organization of the working groups, probably needs more explanation. The Tavistock Institute of Human Relations has done a number of studies in different methods of organizing work. Dr A. T. M. Wilson summarizing some of their research suggests that how work is organized is often less determined by technological factors than might appear; that in designing work organization more attention needs to be given to social factors if the best results are to be obtained in productivity and workers' satisfaction. The research has traced a trend away from one set of principles of work organization to another. He says the following, formerly widespread principles, now appear to be less appropriate to current industrial situations:

(a) maximal task breakdown; with
(b) repetitive task components;
(c) low skill at operative level;
(d) work organization of an aggregate of parallel operative jobs; and
(e) predominantly disciplinary supervision.

Other methods of organizing work have been shown to result in both greater productivity and higher job satisfaction. These are based on the following principles:

(a) overlapping and complementary roles in
(b) structured work groups with

(c) wider or increased operative skill;
(d) increased group responsibility,
(e) internal group leadership, and
(f) increased technical-advisory components in supervision.[27]

Therefore, when management is planning changes in the organization of work it should consider if it can do the following: increase the content of the job, provide more overlapping of work within the individual work group, give the group greater responsibility, and encourage the supervisor to emphasize the technical and advisory aspect of his job. In sum, to give the individual groups greater responsibility for the work in which all can share, rather than each having a small self-contained job.

A case study of a well-planned change, which was successfully introduced, will illustrate how a change can be planned so as to lessen its effect on people. John Smith has described a study he made for the Acton Society of London Transport's conversion of South London tram services to buses in the years 1950–52.[28] This involved replacing 800 trams by buses and transferring and retraining 6,000 tram employees, as well as building work. The conversion which was planned to take two years was completed three months ahead of schedule. During this time there was only one (unofficial) stoppage of work, which only involved 70 maintenance workers and lasted a few hours. More than 1,900 of the 2,000 tram drivers qualified as bus drivers.

The reputation of London Transport as a good employer, supported by a guarantee that no man who had been in the service of the Board on 1 January, 1948, would lose his job or be worse off as a result of the reorganization, contributed to the success of the change, so did direct involvement of local representatives in the joint discussions on the mechanics and problems of conversion. Central recruitment, by cut-

27. Wilson, A. T. M., 'Some Contrasting Socio-Technical Production Systems', *The Manager*, vol. 23, no. 12, pp. 979–86, British Institute of Management, London, December 1955.

28. Smith, J. H., 'Social Aspects of Industrial Change', *Occupational Psychology*, vol. 27, no. 2, pp. 80–8, April 1953.

ting off external recruitment and by close liaison with the receiving departments, enabled displaced tram-men to be placed in other departments. The higher pay and better physical conditions of busmen naturally helped to make the change more acceptable. The design and execution of the training scheme also contributed to the success of the change for it led to a high success rate in training tram drivers as bus drivers, although many of them were over 60 years of age. 'If a man failed, but showed the slightest adaptability, he was allowed to come back a second, or even a third, time until he qualified, or until both he and his instructors were satisfied that there was no purpose in continuing further.' The local representatives consulted regularly with the training officers and visited the training centre to discuss individual cases, so that later they even suggested a change of instructor and gave their views as to which one would be most suitable.

Research on change shows that those who are likely to be affected by it should be told of what is planned and be consulted about what should be done, so that they may have a chance to have a say in how and when the changes which will affect them are introduced. How valuable consultation on change can be in enlisting workers' participation was shown in an experiment carried out by Coch and French in a sewing factory employing about 600 people. The workers were paid by piece rates based on time study. In the past the firm had met strong resistance when it changed production schedules and methods; during the change-over periods production dropped, immediately and markedly, and frequently did not recover completely. There was also a high labour turnover and generally low morale. The experiment consisted of adopting a different method of introducing the change in each of three groups. The first group used the traditional method in which top management issued an instruction to make the change and the workers and their immediate supervisors did not participate in the planning. The second group participated in the plan through representatives. In the third, all members participated. Production dropped initially in all groups, but much less in the third one. It also recovered much more rapidly in this group. The first, or non-participation, group showed no significant improvement of production during the first 40 days after the change-over. During this time 17 per cent of the group left compared with none in the other two groups. The first group also complained about the payment system and about individual managers, complaints which were not made by the other groups.[29]

So far we have talked about resistance to change on the shop floor and what can be done about it, but changes at any level can cause problems. The effects of rapid change on the organization of management can be far-reaching and, unless this is realized, may result in inefficiency as well as frustration and strain. We saw in Chapter 2 that a company in a changing situation will need a much more flexible type of management structure than one that is carrying out well-known and well-defined tasks. The study by Burns and Stalker, referred to earlier,[30] of the effects of change on the managers in a number of established Scottish firms which entered the electronic industry, showed that it had important effects. It increased the frequency of personal contact between managers, which varied directly with the extent to which each firm was undergoing technical changes. It made the boundaries of the manager's job more fluid, so that they could not be set down in detailed job-descriptions or prescribed by rules. Hence, the status that went with the job also became more indefinite, a man's prestige no longer depended upon his title, but upon how he showed up in the frequent discussion made necessary by change and under the pressure resulting from change.[31] Some companies give recognition to the change in the nature of the manager's jobs in such conditions, by establishing temporary problem-

29. Coch, L., and French, J. R. P., 'Overcoming Resistance to Change', *Human Relations*, vol. 1, pp. 512–32, Tavistock Publications, London, 1948.

30. See p. 49.

31. Croome, Honor, op. cit., p. 17.

solving groups, which may consist of people from different parts and levels of the organization, who work together as an equal team with a chairman.

The fact that in a changing situation a man cannot rely on his position for his status can be a source of anxiety for some managers, who dislike uncertainty as to where they stand. We saw in Chapter 7 that a man's tolerance of ambiguity can be an important factor in his success as a manager. Managers whose tolerance is low will feel insecure under the constant challenge of fluid rather than structured or prescribed relationships. If the company is one where management rivalries are intense, rapid change may bring them to the fore as managers will no longer be able to retreat to their own defined jobs for protection – or if they seek to do so, as they may, so much the worse for the success of the change.

Honor Croome in her digest of Burns and Stalker's study suggested two don'ts and two do's in times of rapid technical change which are an admirable summary of the lessons of this and other research into the human aspects of change. Without them technical progress will founder, even though the firm has excellent laboratories and equipment and takes great trouble to recruit good scientists and technologists. Don't blame the troubles that arise on personal cussedness, they may contribute, but there are deeper causes. Don't 'scurry back for safety to the "mechanical" system, the authority of the chief and the book of rules. It is totally inappropriate'. Do constantly re-examine what the firm is supposed to be doing and how it is doing it, with the aim of adopting whatever seems the most appropriate methods and structure. Do emphasize common tasks, both for the company as a whole and for individual groups, rather than separate jobs. Finally, do seek to encourage an atmosphere in which cooperative relationships can flourish, rather than one in which people seek to score points or to assert prestige.[32] The greater the change, the more important become

32. Croome, Honor, 'Human Problems of Innovation', *Problems of Progress in Industry* – 5, pp. 34–5, Department of Scientific and Industrial Research, HMSO, London, 1960.

human relations in determining its success or failure, hence the greater the need for the manager to understand human resistance to change.

SUMMARY

We looked first at the major sources of change affecting management and at what could be done to meet them successfully. Much of our discussion concerned planning for innovation. We noted, in particular, that the increase in information technology may reduce the scope for judgement at middle management level. We also saw that innovation is increasing the proportion of managers and specialists. In consequence, the problems of managing the knowledge worker should be, as Peter Drucker suggests, one of the main fields of study today.

Change, to be successful, must be carefully planned. Such planning must also include the likely human effects of the change and what can be done to ease adjustment to them. In such planning managers can benefit from a knowledge of the most common causes of resistance to change. One of the greatest is fear. Much of it may be unnecessary and result from uncertainty and misapprehension. Some of it may be a reflection of the individual's unconscious fears triggered off by what is seen as a threat to his security.

Resistance to change often comes from social barriers, of which the most important are the rigidities between occupations. Change may destroy a long-established relationship between occupations. For the individual this can mean a loss in the value of his training and experience, and with them a decline in his status. Therefore, resistance to change is often bound up with ideas of status. Another social barrier to change is the attitude to mobility. Many British workers are reluctant to move their homes, although more willing to change their occupations.

There is sufficient evidence to show that much can be done to reduce resistance to change at all levels. The two studies we quoted showed how careful planning and the involvement of the workers, or their representatives, in details of the plan which affect them, can do a great deal to enlist the workers' cooperation. Care should also be given to the method of work organization, which can be either a source of satisfaction or dissatisfaction.

We saw that rapid change can transform the nature of the manager's job, making it more fluid in terms of both responsibilities and status. The successful manager will learn to live with, and to enjoy, the uncertainties that this will cause. He will be ready to search for the methods and the structure that are most suitable to the company's situation. When things go wrong he will look for causes rather than finding scapegoats. Above all, he will see change as an opportunity for cooperative and questing endeavour in which all are involved.

Selected Bibliography

1. FOR THE MANAGER'S OWN USE
These are short and readable.

ACTON SOCIETY TRUST. *Management Initiative.* The Trust, London (pamphlet), 1961.
Case studies of what management did that helped or hindered major changes in the companies analysed.

ARGYRIS, CHRIS. *Personality and Organization: The Conflict Between System and Individual.* Harper & Bros., New York, 1957.
A forceful argument about the effects of the traditional organization on the worker.

BRANTON, NOEL. *Introduction to the Theory and Practice of Management.* Chatto and Windus, London, 1960.

BROWN, J. A. C. *The Social Psychology of Industry.* Penguin Books, Harmondsworth, Mddx., 1954.

BROWN, WILFRED. *Exploration in Management.* Heinemann, London, 1960.
Provocative and original.

CROOME, HONOR. 'Human Problems of Innovation' based on a study by Tom Burns and G. M. Stalker. *Problems of Progress in Industry, No. 5.* Department of Scientific and Industrial Research (pamphlet), HMSO, 1960.
A *must* for any manager in a changing company.

DRUCKER, PETER F. *The Practice of Management.* Heinemann, London, 1955, and Harper & Bros., New York, 1954.
Not short, but worth it.

HOOPER, SIR FREDERICK. *Management Survey.* Penguin Books, Harmondsworth, Mddx., 1960.
An exceptionally well-written book by one of Britain's leading managers.

McGREGOR, DOUGLAS. *The Human Side of Enterprise.* McGraw-Hill, New York (London, 1960).
A *must* for every manager.

STEWART, ROSEMARY. 'Managers for Tomorrow'. *Problems of Progress in Industry, No. 2.* Department of Scientific and Industrial Research, HMSO (pamphlet), 1957.

A short version of the Acton Society Trust's *Management Succession*.

UNIVERSITY OF LIVERPOOL, Department of Social Science. 'Men, Steel and Technical Change.' *Problems of Progress in Industry, No. 1.* Department of Scientific and Industrial Research, HMSO (pamphlet), 1957.

WOODWARD, JOAN. 'Management and Technology.' *Problems of Progress in Industry, No. 3.* Department of Scientific and Industrial Research, HMSO, 1958.

2. *FOR MANAGEMENT TRAINING COURSES*

ABEGGLEN, JAMES C. *The Japanese Factory: Aspects of its Social Organization.* The Free Press, Glencoe, Ill., 1958.

ACTON SOCIETY TRUST. *Size and Morale: a preliminary study of attendance at work in large and small units.* The Trust, London (pamphlet), 1953.

ACTON SOCIETY TRUST. *Size and Morale Part II: A further study of attendance at work in large and small units.* The Trust, London (pamphlet). 1957.

ACTON SOCIETY TRUST. *Management Succession.* The Trust, London, 1956.

BARNARD, CHESTER. *The Functions of the Executive.* Harvard University Press, Cambridge, Mass., 1958 (originally published 1938), Oxford University Press.

BRECH, E. F. L. *Organization: The Framework of Management.* Longmans, Green, London, 1957.

BURNS, TOM, & STALKER, GEORGE M. *Management of Innovation.* Tavistock Publications Ltd, London, 1961.

CARLSON, SUNE. *Executive Behaviour: A Study of the Work Load and the Working Methods of Managing Directors.* Strombergs, Stockholm, 1951.

CLEGG, H. A. *A New Approach to Industrial Democracy.* Basil Blackwell, Oxford, 1960.

EDWARDS, RONALD S. & TOWNSEND, HARRY. Business *Enterprise: Its Growth and Organization.* Macmillan, London, 1958.

HARBISON, FREDERICK, & MYERS, CHARLES A. *Management in the Industrial World: An International Analysis.* McGraw-Hill, New York, 1959.

JAQUES, ELLIOT. *Changing Culture of a Factory.* Tavistock Publications, London, 1951.

JAQUES, ELLIOT. *Measurement of Responsibility: A Study of Work Payment and Individual Capacity*. Tavistock Publications Ltd, London, 1956.

LEAVITT, HAROLD J. *Managerial Psychology*. University Press, Chicago, 1958.

LIKERT, RENSIS. *New Patterns of Management*. McGraw-Hill, New York, 1961.

MAYO, ELTON. *Social Problems of an Industrial Civilization*. Harvard University Press, Cambridge, Mass., 1945.

PFIFFNER, JOHN M., & SHERWOOD, FRANK P. *Administrative Organization*. PrenticeHall, Englewood Cliffs, NJ (London, 1960).
One of the best of the many American compilations. This one discusses different research, instead of just extracting chapters from other books.

SHARTLE, CARROLL L. *Executive Performance and Leadership*. Staples Press, London, 1957.

SIMON, HERBERT A. *Administrative Behaviour*. Macmillan, New York (second edition), 1957.

URWICK, LYNDALL. *Notes on the Theory of Organization*. American Management Association, New York, 1952.

URWICK, L. F. *The Pattern of Management*. Pitman, London, 1956.

WALKER, CHARLES R., & GUEST, ROBERT H. *The Foreman on the Assembly Line*. Harvard University Press, Cambridge, Mass., 1952.

WHYTE, WILLIAM H., JR, and the Editors of *Fortune*. *Is Anybody Listening?* Simon & Schuster, New York, 1952.

WHYTE, WILLIAM H., JR, *The Organization Man*. Simon & Schuster, New York, 1956. Jonathan Cape, London, 1957.

Index

MANAGEMENT AND MARKETING SERIES

THE PRACTICE OF MANAGEMENT 10/6

By PETER F. DRUCKER. An outstanding contribution to management theory and practice.

MANAGING FOR RESULTS 7/6

By PETER F. DRUCKER. A 'what to do' book for the top echelons of management.

PLANNED MARKETING 6/-

By RALPH GLASSER. A lucid introduction to mid-Atlantic marketing techniques.

CAREERS IN MARKETING 6/-

By THE INSTITUTE OF MARKETING. A guide for those seeking a job in the exciting field of marketing.

GUIDE TO SAMPLING 6/-

By MORRIS JAMES SLONIM. A fine exposition of sampling theory and techniques.

INNOVATION IN MARKETING 7/6

By THEODORE LEVITT. A brilliant exposition of original and stimulating ideas on modern approaches to marketing.

MAKING MANPOWER EFFECTIVE (Part 1) 7/6

By JAMES J. LYNCH. The techniques of company manpower planning and forecasting.

THE REALITY OF MANAGEMENT 6/-

By ROSEMARY STEWART. Compass bearings to help the manager plot his career.

DYNAMIC BUSINESS MANAGEMENT 5/-

By HAROLD NORCROSS. A simple guide to the rudiments of successful business management.

BUSINESS PLANNING 8/6

By D.R.C. HALFORD. An absorbing and stimulating analysis of planning in all its faces.

PAN PIPER SCIENCE SERIES

'This excellent paperback science series which aims to keep pace with the bewildering advances in the scientific world provides thoroughly stimulating reading for the layman'   Bristol Evening Post

---

PLASTICS, RUBBERS AND FIBRES:
MATERIALS FOR MAN'S USE   5/- illus.

By LAWRENCE W. CHUBB. How man has converted raw materials into a substance indispensable to our civilization.

PLASTICS AND YOU   5/- illus.

By ROGER LUSHINGTON. How plastics have become vital in the home, in industry, clothing, transport and building; including a complete glossary of all types of plastics on the market.

ANIMAL NAVIGATION   5/- illus.

By R. M. LOCKLEY. How sight, smell, hearing, touch, etc., as well as some obscure and little-understood senses, are used by animals in their everyday life.

MENTAL DISORDER:
A PROBLEM WITH MANY FACETS   5/-

By MAN MOHAN SINGH, MB, BS, (DPM RCP Lond., RCS Eng.)

Psychiatric theory from the beginning of its discovery until the present day.

THE BASIC FACTS OF HUMAN HEREDITY
6/- illus.

By AMRAM SCHEINFELD. Can diseases be inherited? What will your children look like? Can mental diseases and abnormalities be passed on? These and many other fascinating questions are all clearly explained.

A COMPACT SCIENCE DICTIONARY   6/-

Edited by G. E. SPECK, revised by Bernard Jaffe.

Authoritative, up-to-date, encyclopaedic guide to the world of modern science.